THE NONRESIDENTIAL MISSIONARY

V. David Garrison

INNOVATIONS IN MISSION

Bryant L. Myers, Series Editor

THE NONRESIDENTIAL MISSIONARY
A new strategy and the people it serves

V. David Garrison

The Nonresidential Missionary is the first in MARC's Innovations in Mission series. This volume is published jointly by MARC and New Hope, P. O. Box 11657, Birmingham, Alabama, 35202 USA. Maps courtesy of Global Mapping International, 1605 East Elizabeth Street, Pasadena, California 91104 USA.

ISBN: 0-912552-71-9

Printed in the United States of America. First printing: November 1990. Second printing: September 1992. Cover Design: Edler Graphics, Monrovia, California. Typography: Ventura Publisher. Body text: Palatino 12.5 pts, reduced photographically to 82%.

AUTHOR'S ACKNOWLEDGMENT

I am indebted to my many colleagues at the Foreign
Mission Board who assisted in the development of this
book at every stage. My deepest admiration goes to
those pioneering nonresidential missionaries who have
taken a concept and turned it into reality. Finally, I
want to thank the ones who have made the greatest
sacrifice for the development of this idea, program and
book: my wife Sonia, my son Jeremiah, and my
daughter Seneca.

INTRODUCTION TO A NEW SERIES

WELCOME TO MARC'S NEW SERIES, *Innovations in Mission*. The 1990's are a time of rapid change in almost every area of life. Political and economic maps are being redrawn. Technology is advancing at a dizzying pace. The center of gravity of Christ's body in the world has shifted to the southern hemisphere. The church is exploding in China and on the Pacific Rim. Theology of mission is being written at the grassroots among the poor. The cost of misusing and abusing God's creation is staring us in the face.

In the midst of this climate of rapid change, extreme complexity and almost obsessive pluralism, the church of Jesus Christ is to be in mission. The good news of Jesus Christ and the claims of his Kingdom are needed everywhere.

Post-Christian Europe needs to rediscover the gospel that was once central to its culture and sense of being. The nomadic pastoralists—living across the Sahel in Africa, throughout the Middle East, in the eastern provinces of the USSR and in western and southern China—need to hear a gospel "that will fit on the back of a camel." The poor in Latin America need a gospel that restores their relationship with God and reverses the erosion of their quality of life. North Americans need to hear good news that restores the vibrancy of worship and commitment to change their culturally captive forms of Christianity. The rich and powerful everywhere need to hear how difficult it is for them to get in the Kingdom of Heaven.

MARC is in the business of inspiring vision and motivating mission among those who are taking the whole gospel to the whole world. One of the ways we seek to fulfill our mission is to identify and share the stories of innovations in mission which, in our fallible view, make sense in this kind of changing, chaotic world. We seek to broadcast what we have discovered as good news in mission in hopes that others might find this information useful in enhancing their own mission. This series, *Innovations in Mission*, is the tool we have chosen for sharing this information with the global Christian mission community. We hope it will be valuable to mission strategists and executives, mission professors and students, and all those for whom Christian mission is part of living life with Christ.

The Nonresidential Missionary is the story of an innovation in mission that emerged from a creative dialogue between missiologists with the Southern Baptist Foreign Mission Board and the *World Evangelization Database*, both of which are located in Richmond, Virginia. This book invites a wider audience to join the conversation.

The main goal of the nonresidential missionary is to project the good news of Jesus Christ beyond barriers and restrictions, so that those who have not yet heard will have the chance to respond. To do this, he or she has to live somewhere other than in the midst of the people, city or geographical area to be served.

This exciting new approach takes advantage of recent technology and access to large amounts of diverse information and puts them at the service of those carrying out Christian mission in such challenging places. The nonresidential missionary seeks partnership and cooperation between the diverse members of Christ's body. We believe this innovative approach is a breakthrough in missions strategy in the 1990s. We hope you will agree.

Bryant L. Myers
Series Editor

TABLE OF CONTENTS

LIST OF TABLES AND MAPS

TABLES

MAPS

INTRODUCTION

NONRESIDENTIAL MISSION IS ONE OF THE MOST recent in a long history of innovative approaches to world evangelization. Casual hearers or readers, upon first encountering the term, often assume that they know its meaning, and generally envision something akin to an itinerant missionary or perhaps even a missionary on furlough. I hope that this book will serve to clarify and lend substance to a concept that first appeared in 1986.

Nonresidential mission holds particular promise in an age when the world's nearly 1.8 billion Christians remain frustrated by the persistent challenge of roughly a quarter of the earth's inhabitants who have yet to hear the gospel of Jesus Christ. Perhaps we find the existence of more than a billion unevangelized people so troubling because of our embarrassment over our own riches. A civilization that can place a spaceship on the moon and propel satellites beyond the solar system should certainly be able to obey Christ's commission to share his message with every fellow human being. The resources are abundant, and yet the task remains undone.

As this book reveals, there are numerous reasons for this discrepancy between abundant resources and great gospel deserts. While obstacles remain to completing the unfinished task, the nonresidential missionary method is uniquely adapted to overcoming these obstacles. By definition, nonresidential missionaries use every conceivable method to bring the gospel to people who have never had the opportunity to respond to it.

Though the nonresidential missionary approach is new, in its brief history it has demonstrated a remarkable capacity to change an evangelistically stagnant situation. The major reason for this is that resources already exist in abundance for sharing the gospel with the whole world. The nonresidential missionary's toolbox is well-stocked. The task is one of redeploying these resources to their greatest strategic advantage. It is for this reason the nonresidential missionary approach is never in competition with any other mission method. Instead, it both presupposes and includes these other ministries as key resources for accomplishing its own objectives. Thus, the healthier and more diverse the world of Christian mission resources becomes, the more vital the nonresidential missionary approach will be.

In attempting to explain this innovative approach to candidates and constituents over the years, I have become increasingly aware of the value of using illustrations of "real life" nonresidential missionary work. Again and again, we have seen that the concept and vision of nonresidential missions is more caught than taught. All further instruction is secondary once an individual has caught the vision of reaching an unevangelized people or cities, gaining access to all the vast resources of the Christian world, and weaving them into one holistic mission strategy.

It is not an exaggeration to say that the nonresidential missionary is limited only by his or her own imagination. In hope of kindling this kind of enterprising spirit, graphic "slices of life" from actual nonresidential missionary ministries have been interspersed throughout this work.

This approach cannot be completely understood by viewing it from a single perspective or in an isolated setting. Like the world it seeks to reach, the nonresidential missionary method is complex and diverse. Accordingly, it must be examined under various lights and in a variety of contexts to appreciate fully its uniqueness. For this reason, I have attempted to present the work of the nonresidential missionary in various ways. In Part One of this book, the ministry is examined in a simple definition, through its historical origins and determinants; in its biblical basis; in a catalogue of its characteristics, and perhaps most significantly, in a collection of actual vignettes describing how it is at work today throughout the world.

Part Two attempts to give the reader a handle on the parts of the world that have limited or no access to Christian witness. The world's least evangelized nations, cities, and peoples are listed, and organized into twelve ethnographic groups. These twelve groups are provided so that Christians hoping to serve a particular people can begin to build a network with others called to socio-culturally related peoples. Again, it is hoped that the vignettes used in Part One will inspire readers to take responsibility for an unevangelized population segment in one of these twelve groups.

Each of the "case studies" is set in a different part of the world, and highlights a different aspect of the nonresidential missionary's work. By viewing this type of mission from the perspectives of European, Latin American, Asian and North American missionaries, as well as through the eyes of those who have been reached by their efforts, the tremendous potential held forth by this approach becomes apparent.

Every illustration corresponds to an actual effort used by a nonresidential missionary somewhere in the world to share the gospel with those who have never heard it. In each illustration, however, names have been changed and locations obscured so that ministries currently in progress will not be hindered. I hope that readers will understand the sensitive nature of working in places where, for a variety of reasons, overt and explicit evangelistic activity is not allowed. Someday the stories will all be told in full. And that day will be one of great rejoicing.

David Garrison
October 15, 1990

## PART ONE

A NEW STRATEGY

## ONE

Mission beyond barriers

IT WAS A BITTERLY COLD JANUARY NIGHT in Kazar, the ancient Turkestani capital of the Bashkaz Autonomous Region, situated nearly a thousand miles east of Moscow in the direction of Siberia. Four men cloaked in long woolen overcoats and gray Russian fur caps emerged from the back of an oversized black Volga sedan. Leading the entourage through the broad streets of the city was a tall middle-aged Soviet bureaucrat named Alexi Aitmatov. On his left walked Constantin Abdullayev, the Bashkaz Minister of Foreign Trade, and to his right their translator, Rashid Ulamov. Next to Ulamov walked a young Scotsman from Edinburgh named Michael Knox.[1]

After an obligatory stroll through Lenin Square and Patriot's Park, with its beautiful poplar-lined walkways and garish busts of Karl Marx and Frederick Engels, the four men entered an apartment complex catering exclusively to Party officials. Tonight, their matronly Bashkaz hostess had prepared a banquet of traditional Russian and Bashkaz cuisine to honor their British guest, who had just signed an unprecedented array of protocols and contracts initiating a new level of relationship for trade and educational interchange between the USSR and Great Britain.

Michael Knox is a nonresidential missionary. He came to Kazar with a rudimentary knowledge of the Russian language, a passionate interest in the history of the Bashkaz people and a desire to see the Bashkaz region open to the gospel of Jesus Christ. In the course of his research into the Turkic peoples of the Bashkaz region, he learned a great deal: there was no intelligible translation of the Bible in their language; no Christian agency was transmitting the gospel to the Bashkaz through radio programs; and no Christians from outside the Soviet Union were attempting to reach this people.

---

1   The nonresidential ministries described in this chapter have actually taken place somewhere in the unevangelized world. Identities, population target and details have all been altered to protect those involved.

Not all that Michael Knox discovered was negative, however. Russian Pentecostal Christians in Kazar had begun praying for and reaching out to their Bashkaz neighbors. Also, since 1982, when a Soviet trade delegation first came to Great Britain, a "city-to-city" friendship had been established between the cities of Birmingham, England, and Kazar, Bashkazestan.

Little had come from the trade and cultural protocols signed between the two cities until 1989, when Knox determined to use the city-to-city avenue as a means of proclamation. He spent six months organizing a dozen churches in Birmingham to pray for the Bashkaz people. He then worked through a local university and two secondary schools to catalyze interest in a student exchange program. By the time Knox entered Kazar in January of 1990, scores of Christians had been praying for months for the evangelization of the Bashkaz and more than a dozen families had committed either to send or to receive students in a Bashkaz-Birmingham educational exchange program.

Knox had high hopes for this exchange program. If all went according to schedule, nearly one hundred Christians from the U.K. and several other non-Communist countries would be living and sharing their faith in Bashkazestan within a year. An equal number of Bashkazi would be living in the homes of evangelical Christians in Birmingham—Christians who had learned about the Bashkazi and had been praying for them for nearly a year.

After finishing the banquet with his Soviet hosts, Knox returned to his hotel room, and began preparing for his return to England and the busy events which would dominate his schedule in the weeks and months ahead. In three days, he would reunite with his family in London and begin making arrangements for a delegation of Christian businessmen to follow up on the invitation he had received from the Minister of Foreign Trade to return to Kazar in the spring. The new Soviet policies of *glasnost* and *perestroika* perfectly complemented Knox's plans to expand the flow of persons and ideas into this long-restricted region.

From their flat in Surrey, just south of London, Michael's wife Sarah would relate the good news of his Kazar trip not only to his co-workers in Birmingham, but also to a network of evangelical student organizations in countries around the world. From these ranks, the Knoxes hoped to raise up an international team of Christian co-laborers to join in bringing the good news to Bashkazestan.

After two and a half years of nonresidential ministry to the Bashkazi, Knox has already seen great progress toward the evangelization of his people. But he knows that the work is really just beginning. Many years of faithful effort must ensue before the Bashkazi can be said to have been given a fair chance to hear and respond to the gospel of Jesus Christ. The Knoxes welcome the challenge.

The Latino-Berber connection in France

On a busy side street in the crowded Arab quarter of a city in the South of France, a young Latin American couple from Costa Rica—Rafael and Miriam Gaxiola—wait for their language tutors to help them in the rigors of a North African Berber language called Jebala. Soon they are joined by two North African companions, and they set out through the busy streets of the city a few blocks north of the *Museé du Sacreceour*.

Rafael and Miriam are nonresidential missionaries; their tutors are Berber Christians from North Africa. The younger of the two is named Emir—a slender, handsome man in his mid-twenties with Middle Eastern features and warm green eyes. The older man is named Majid. Majid is in his late forties, as evidenced by his silvering black hair and creased forehead. Emir and Majid are from the Jebala region of North Africa's mountainous interior.

The Berbers of North Africa are the aboriginal inhabitants of the region. Since at least the second millennium B.C., their ancestors have settled the lands stretching from modern-day Libya to the Atlantic coast of Western Sahara. Over the centuries they have witnessed numerous visitations and conquests by outsiders. Seafaring Phoenicians, Imperial Romans, German Vandals, Byzantine Greeks and Bedouin Arabs each left their mark. All eventually left, except for the Arabs, who remained to rule the nations of North Africa for more than a thousand years. To retain their culture against Arab assimilation, many Berbers were forced to retreat to the mountains. Here they have eked out a difficult existence which continues to the present. The Berbers call themselves *imazighen*, which means "free men."

The Gaxiolas have come to love and admire the Berbers' commitment to freedom and self-expression. At the same time, they have seen how the Berbers' isolation in the mountains of North Africa has separated them from the Gospel of Jesus Christ. Yet through their nonresidential approach, the Gaxiolas have been able to reach Berbers like Emir and Majid with the good news.

Emir's pilgrimage bears a similarity to that of many Berbers from North Africa. When he was twenty years old, he was sent to France to live with his aunt and uncle and work in their coffee house. For Emir, France was a new world filled with boundless possibilities, but also with loneliness.

One summer afternoon as he walked along the boulevard, Emir met two young women visiting France on summer vacation from a university in Latin America. One of the young women boldly asked

Emir if she could tell him about Jesus Christ. Emir was surprised, but quickly consented. She told him how she had turned to Christ as a college freshman in Mexico City, and how Christ had forgiven her sins and given her a new direction in life. Then she told Emir how Christ could come into his life as well, bringing the forgiveness and liberation from sin and guilt that he needed.

Emir did not know how to respond to this sincere young witness, but he thanked the two young women for talking with him. Before they left him, one of them gave him a pocket-sized French New Testament and a gospel tract with the address of a local Christian bookstore.

What Emir could not have known at the time was that the two women were part of a group of 25 college students from Mexico City and San Jose, Costa Rica, who were spending their summer vacation reaching out to some of France's more than 2 million North African Muslims. Their invitation, organization and orientation had been developed in cooperation with two student mission agencies, and guided by the Gaxiolas. This team of young witnesses was an integral part of the Gaxiolas' effort to reach the Jebala Berbers of North Africa through Christian ministry to Berbers in Europe.

Two weeks later, Emir sat alone in his room reading from the little New Testament he had been given. Shortly before midnight he fell asleep, still wrestling with the words from St. John's Gospel: "I am the way, the truth, and the life; no one comes to the Father but by me." Later that night, Emir was visited in his sleep by a vision of Christ standing at the foot of his bed. As the vision faded, Emir awakened. He interpreted the vision to be a sign from Allah revealing to him the truth about his son. That night, Emir invited Christ into his life.

The next morning, after finishing work at the coffee house, Emir set out to find the bookstore advertised in the gospel tract he had received. There he met Majid, the proprietor of the only Berber Christian bookstore in the city. A warm bond of Christian fellowship followed. Emir was baptized into the little community of Jebala Christians who met each Sunday night in the back of the bookstore. After their meetings, the believers would typically linger for hours drinking coffee and discussing with the Gaxiolas their vision to serve the Berbers.

Majid had also come to Christ through the efforts of a nonresidential ministry. In his case, the ministry had touched him while he was still living in North Africa, in the form of a Jebala radio broadcast. Listening to his radio one night, Majid's attention was captured by the sole radio program in his mother tongue. All others were either in Arabic or some European language. The program was about the life of Isa (Jesus) the Messiah. Majid followed the program for several weeks before a particular message touched his heart. Quietly and alone, Majid invited Christ into his life and accepted God's forgiveness through him.

The Gaxiolas had played a crucial role in developing the Jebala radio program that so touched Majid and many others living in North Africa. Because of their nonresidential vantage point in Europe, the Gaxiolas were able to remain in close contact with the radio station that had issued the broadcast. As letters of response arrived from Jebala listeners, Miriam and Rafael plotted the location of their return addresses on a map of North Africa. They moved down the list of a network of Christians living in North Africa, asking each to make contact with inquirers in their communities and to incorporate them into local churches.

Majid became a Christian and was discipled by tentmakers contacted through the Gaxiolas' network. Later, when local persecution forced Majid to leave North Africa and flee to France, friends used the same network to alert the Gaxiolas. They were able to meet him at the airport and help him begin a new life sharing his faith with the Berber people there.

Emir and Majid have become partners with the Gaxiolas in a concert of Jebala evangelization that grows more intricate with each passing month. Miriam has extended the effort to include networks of believers from around the world. During her nonresidential training in Costa Rica, Miriam developed skills in word processing, database management and electronic communications through an American telephone company's telecommunications system.

Since that time, she has expanded her skills to include desktop publishing. She now publishes a newsletter called *The Jebala Journal*, a quarterly bulletin of Jebala news, prayer needs, and ministry opportunities. Using a multi-lingual font package, she prints the bulletin in four languages: English, French, Spanish and Portuguese. She and Rafael hope eventually to create the type needed to print the *Journal* in Jebala as well.

Using the telecommunications system, Miriam sends news of urgent needs to her brother, Manuel, a pastor in Costa Rica. Manuel spreads news of prayer needs and opportunities for witness to a network of churches throughout the country. An even more diverse network is informed when Miriam sends news bulletins to the COM-IBAM (Congreso Misionero Ibero-Americano) office in Sao Paolo, Brazil. From this evangelical communications hub, information on Jebala needs and opportunities immediately goes to 20 cooperating mission agencies. Through these channels and others like them in the United States, Rafael and Miriam have organized annual student evangelism projects in France each summer that have resulted in nearly 100 conversions over the past three years.

In North Africa itself, Rafael has used his rapid communications system to place five Christian tentmakers from Costa Rica, Brazil and Argentina in jobs within the North African interior where they have daily contact with Jebala people. Miriam and Rafael hope to place dozens of Christian witnesses like these in North Africa among the Berbers over the next few years. Already the small team of witnesses there have led seven Jebala to Christ, and are teaching these seven to share their faith with others.

Rafael and Miriam are only beginning to make a dent in the awesome challenge of Jebala evangelization, but they know they are making a difference. Already, a young couple from Brazil have come for two summers to the evangelism projects in France with plans to give their life to reaching the Jebala people. One of the tentmakers in North Africa, a zealous believer from Argentina, has also caught the vision of reaching the Jebala with the gospel. The secret behind Rafael and Miriam's hope is in their conviction that Christ wills and desires that the Jebala know him, and in their knowledge that they are not alone in this effort. Ongoing prayer for the Jebala by hundreds of prayer partners will assure a continued influx of co-laborers, each making a unique contribution to the mosaic of Jebala evangelization.

Defining our terms

AS A NEW CONCEPT WITH DISTINCT CHARACTERISTICS, the nonresidential missionary is often confused with other types of missionary methods that approximate some of its many aspects. While it is difficult to encompass all of the diverse components of a nonresidential missionary's profile into a concise definition, the following paragraphs attempt this very thing. The words used to define and discuss nonresidential mission in this chapter and throughout the rest of this book may require precise technical definitions or may be unfamiliar to the reader. Several of these are included in a glossary in Appendix Three.

A more exhaustive definition than the one given below is in Appendix One, *An expanded definition*. For purposes of a foundational working definition, however, the following should suffice.

Nonresidential mission in a nutshell

A nonresidential missionary is a full-time, professional career foreign missionary who is matched up with a single unevangelized population segment (see *Glossary*) for purposes of concentrating on priorities of initial evangelization and eliminating gaps and inadvertent duplications with other agencies.

The nonresidential missionary lives outside the targeted assignment because legal residence for a missionary is either prohibited or highly restricted. From this nonresidential base, he or she networks with all other concerned Christians (denominations, agencies and individuals), both local and non-local, to do the following:

1. Research and survey the situation of that single population segment, becoming expert in the subject for purposes of evangelization and ministry;

2. Become fluent in that population's main language;

3. Draw up and help to see implemented a wide range of evangelizing ministry options directed towards that population by persistently advocating the evangelization of the population before the world's host of Christian resources;

4. Report regularly to a home office outlining progress with that population, in order to monitor progress and receive assistance as needed;

5. Relate to resource networks like the *World Evangelization Database* made available to mission agencies by the Foreign Mission Board of the Southern Baptist Convention; and

6. Relate as part of a global team to other nonresidential missionaries, each of whom has been assigned to a different population segment.

The overarching objective of the nonresidential missionary is to see to it that through the whole vast network of Christian influences all persons in his population segment are given an opportunity to respond to Jesus Christ. Also, at least a beachhead church (see *Glossary*) should be planted among that population by A.D. 2000.

The final words in this rather thorough definition link the non-residential missionary's task to the end of the millennium. This very deliberate association is more pragmatic than apocalyptic. The year 2000 represents an unprecedented focal date for hundreds of Christian denominations and mission agencies. For the nonresidential mission-ary, this global consensus provides the resource bank needed to bring about the first stage of the overall goal—that every person in the population segment might hear and be able to respond to the gospel of Jesus Christ. The year 2000 also underscores the concrete task of the nonresidential missionary. It is neither unattainable nor immeasurable, but an accountable undertaking demanding that clearly defined steps be taken toward its fulfillment.

Out of this complex definition, three essential characteristics emerge:

1. The nonresidential missionary operates fundamentally from a nonresidential base.

2. He or she builds networks with all other similarly concerned Christians.

3. He or she takes responsibility for the evangelization of a single, predominantly unevangelized population segment.

Working from the outside

Working from a nonresidential base means the missionary does not establish a base of operations among the people. While it may be possible and even beneficial for the nonresidential missionary to live among or near the people for purposes of language acquisition and investigation, the real work begins after he or she withdraws to an unrestricted setting in a world-class or crossroads city. The primary reason for nonresidence is due to restrictions placed on a missionary living among the people. In many cases, where it may be possible for clandestine or tentmaking missionaries to live with the people, restrictions prohibit them from implementing the range of options needed to reach the entire population.

Unlike an itinerant missionary or a Bible smuggler, the nonresidential missionary is not necessarily committed to living as close as possible to the borders where the people live. Instead, he or she looks for a strategic place of residence that will allow maximum networking capabilities with other concerned Christians. Some important factors to consider in the decision are:

1. Free flow of information (computers, telecommunications, telephone, postal, etc.);
2. Clusters of key agencies and individuals with resources relevant to the assignment;
3. Proximity to an expatriate community of the target segment (refugees, migrant workers, etc.); and
4. Location along a key travel route in and out of the region (for airplanes, trains, etc.).

Working in partnership

Rather than trying to make all of the primary contacts himself, the nonresidential missionary relies on hundreds of other individuals and agencies. This underscores the second distinctive characteristic of a nonresidential missionary: building networks with all other similarly concerned Christian agencies and individuals.

It is inconceivable for a nonresidential missionary to attempt either a "lone-ranger" approach to evangelizing his population target or even a "mono-denominational" approach. The challenges of presenting the gospel to a highly restricted people are far too difficult to undertake without a full array of resources. Even the largest American Protestant denomination, the Southern Baptist Convention—with nearly 15 million constituents—pales in comparison to the enormity of reaching 1.3 billion lost people. By using every possible Christian contact, rather than a single, limited evangelistic contact, the nonresidential missionary is able to catalyze hundreds—and even thousands—of agents in a concerted effort to serve a specific population segment.

Single-minded focus

By limiting the nonresidential missionary to a single unevangelized population segment, the task is kept both manageable and strategic. While some frontier missions enthusiasts have made it their vocation to call attention to the entire unevangelized world, they have failed to change that world, largely because they refused to limit themselves to a single population segment. Over the years, they are perceived as unfocused, and in the course of time, may actually contribute little to any individual people group coming closer to a saving knowledge of Christ. Their lack of focus allows them to slip conveniently from assignment to assignment whenever an obstacle arises. Accordingly, they remain quite busy, but see little in the way of actual progress from their efforts.

The nonresidential missionary remains committed to a single unevangelized target, faithfully pursuing it in season and out of season, until the day that the task is completed, and its people are capable of pursuing Christ independent of foreign efforts.

Other quasi-nonresidential missionaries utilize the methods of a nonresidential missionary but target peoples which are largely evangelized already or even nominally Christian. Unevangelized population segments are those that have yet to receive an opportunity to hear and respond to the gospel of Jesus Christ. This should not be confused with a closed country, which may or may not be evangelized. Nor should it be equated with a population segment which, though non-Christian, has numerous options for receiving the gospel within its own context. Just as every individual has the God-given right to hear and accept the Gospel, so too have they the right to reject it. The nonresidential concept is grounded on the premise that every person should at least have the opportunity to hear and respond.

Along with these three essential characteristics of non-residential missions are four essential functions: 1) researching; 2) strategizing; 3) implementing; and 4) evaluating.

Research comes first

Research prepares the way for all subsequent work. There are two worlds that the nonresidential missionary must master: the world of the targeted population segment and the world of evangelization resources. Understanding the people is vital, but the toolbox of resources must also be well-stocked. The ultimate goal is to bring these two worlds together in a dynamic interaction, leading to the evangelization of the population target in a manner that will result in healthy, self-propagating churches.

Forming a strategy

After investigating the two worlds, the nonresidential missionary begins developing a comprehensive strategy, which, as much as possible, should cover the entire spectrum of evangelizing options. Four fundamental categories of such a strategy have been identified:

1. Prayer

Each nonresidential missionary has strongly felt the need for a firm foundation of prayer. The least evangelized countries, cities and peoples on earth have long been under the spiritual domination of Satan; only fervent and concerted prayer can break this oppressive control. As people begin to pray for these great unevangelized areas, not only are new doors opened for witness, but God also works a miracle of grace in the hearts of the praying people. Once their hearts are changed by prayer, Christians who never before considered participating in missions begin to discover ways they themselves can participate in reaching out to the ends of the earth.

2. Scripture

There is no limit to the effectiveness of God's Word once it is made available to people who have never heard it. Rochunga Pudaite, President of Bibles for the World, is a Christian from the remote and highly restricted State of Manipur in northeast India. Despite its isolation from missionary witness, Manipur is also one of the most Christianized regions of the entire Indian sub-continent. When asked how people living so far from other Christian centers turned to Christ in such great numbers, Pudaite responded: "Someone sent us a single copy of the Gospel of St. John—we all read it and believed." God's words are powerful. Consequently, nonresidential missionaries place a high premium on providing them to people in their own language.

Most of the world's unevangelized peoples have no recourse to Scripture for one of several reasons. Either the Scriptures are out of print, or they are no longer intelligible (due to linguistic changes), or they are unavailable due to lack of distribution, or they have never been translated in the first place. A crucial part of the nonresidential missionary's initial research is to determine the status of Scripture translation or accessibility, and to devise plans for making it available.

In many cases, the population target may not even have a literate language. In other words, though their mother tongue is widely spoken, it may not be written or read. This has never deterred Christian missionaries from pursuing a Bible translation. More languages throughout the world have been reduced to writing for the first time by a Bible translation than by any other means. Historically, many of these Bible-initiating efforts have spawned entire literary traditions—not to mention great movements toward Christ. Even for an illiterate people, Bible translation is crucial, since there are now numerous ways to present the Bible to people apart from the written word. Radio broadcasts, audio cassette ministries and even video formats such as the "Jesus Film" are all capable of delivering the Scriptures to a people who can understand the spoken though not the written word. However, each of these formats requires a completed Bible translation. Consequently, producing a Bible translation remains a top priority for a nonresidential missionary's strategy.

3. Media Ministries

The use of media ministries is a key method of projecting the Gospel into places where missionary residence is not allowed. Few societies today are without radio receivers, and virtually all nonresidential missionaries depend on radio broadcasts to transmit the gospel into unevangelized hinterlands. Other means of media communication include correspondence evangelism, utilizing both personal correspondence and mass mailings into restricted settings. The remarkably effective "Jesus Film" can now be delivered into highly restricted countries, and reproduced through a number of formats ranging from 8mm films to slides and videocassettes.

4. Christian witnessing presence

To be effective in its goal of evangelism and church planting, each nonresidential ministry must identify opportunities to foster a witnessing Christian presence among the population target. Since traditional missionary presence may be forbidden or highly restricted, the nonresidential mission strategist must rely on non-traditional means of placing a witnessing Christian presence. Once the door is opened to nontraditional possibilities, the nonresidential missionary finds a wide range of options. Even though full-time professional missionaries may not be an option, the goal of evangelism that results in churches remains the same. As one strategist puts it, "Nonresidential missions is just church planting from a nonresidential base."

The creative placement of "front-line" Christian witnesses is a key component in reaching this goal. The following chart is an example of several types of residential witnesses and their lengths of service.

EXAMPLES OF CHRISTIAN WITNESSING PRESENCE

Type	Short-term	Medium-term	Long-term
Mission related	25 English teachers	10 exchange students	3 tentmakers
Relief and development	10 crisis surveyors	15 2-yr relief workers	4 development workers
2/3rd world mission	35 tourist evangelists	3 itinerant evangelists	1 immigrant
Indigenous	30 lay volunteers	12 church planters	2 pastors
TOTAL	100	40	10

In this scheme, long-term workers—though fewer in number and more difficult to secure—provide the type of ongoing presence ministry required to maximize the evangelistic effectiveness of shorter-term personnel. Tourists-evangelists and itinerant evangelists will average only two weeks each in the target area, while the "medium-length" relief and development personnel could stay for as long as two years.

Implementation of this strategy requires careful coordination of goals and action plans with dozens of other Christian agencies and individuals. The nonresidential missionary has only the power of persuasion at this crucial juncture. Also available, however, are literally hundreds of agencies and thousands of individuals from which to recruit.

A key principle behind these efforts is "multi-processing." Multi-processing is a term borrowed from the world of computers, describing how supercomputers use multiple processors to dissect and process extremely complex problems. These multiple and parallel processors work side by side, with the presupposition that dividing the task will not only ensure that it will be solved more quickly, but will also serve as a necessary hedge against the breakdown of individual components. The nonresidential missionary must also build in a certain measure of redundancy, to compensate for shortcomings due to the difficulties of the task and the inevitability of human frailties. By preparing for occasional breakdowns with reliable back-up resources, the missionary's overarching strategy is never frustrated to the point of collapse.

Measuring progress

The work of the nonresidential missionary is not complete without careful monitoring and evaluation of the segment to determine to what extent the various methods are proving effective. Evangelistic effectiveness, or the production of viable self-sustaining and reproducing churches, is the ultimate goal. This effectiveness is monitored by continually examining the conditions of the target segment, using a range of indicators to measure evangelization activity, while upholding the criterion of evangelism that results in churches as the final measure.

Because the nonresidential missionary's task is a dynamic one, there is literally no end to the cycle of studying the situation and resources, devising and implementing new evangelization strategies, monitoring results and refining methods. At the end of each cycle is the beginning of a new, deeper and more extensive array of evangelization efforts.

What a nonresidential missionary is not

Once, when addressing a large group of missionaries and mission strategists on the subject of innovative approaches to closed countries, I asked if there were any nonresidential missionaries in the room. A young fellow in the back eagerly raised his hand. I asked him what country or people he was targeting and he responded, "Mauritania." I was delighted to hear this, and made certain to speak with him after my presentation.

Upon further discussion with the young man, I was disappointed to learn that he was in fact a frustrated residential missionary who had convinced his mission board that he was called to evangelize Mauritania, and was now in the long and frustrating process of waiting for a visa to enter the country. Unable to gain entry, he concluded, "I must be a nonresidential missionary."

But a nonresidential missionary is *not* simply a missionary who cannot get a visa! Differentiating the nonresidential ministry from other kinds of ministry is in no way intended to slight or to discredit the others. It must be noted, however, that a nonresidential missionary is unique, and, while sharing a number of characteristics with other missionary types, must not be confused with them. Short cuts to a complete nonresidential missionary ministry can have seriously debilitating consequences to its effectiveness.

A nonresidential missionary is not a tentmaker, though he may work with dozens or even hundreds of tentmakers to fulfill the scope of his ministry. He may even adopt a tentmaker mode of residence himself temporarily, in order to better learn the language or to negotiate some openings for ministry. The nonresidential missionary realizes, however, that a true tentmaker is committed to a full-time secular job which exists within limits placed on foreigners by the government.

While tentmaker positions are very important within the total scheme of a people's evangelization, they are also quite limiting. A nonresidential missionary remains fundamentally nonresidential, free to mobilize resources and coordinate dozens of projects that a tentmaker's residential restrictions would not allow. At the same time, part of the nonresidential missionary's commitment is to create scores of tentmaker openings and to mobilize an equal number of qualified tentmaker candidates to fill those openings.

A nonresidential missionary is also not a clandestine or illegal missionary. The nonresidential missionary understands the important role clandestine missionaries play, and does not seek to discredit agencies or individuals who do see as their raison d'etre the illicit importation and propagation of the gospel.

Nonresidential missionaries, however, adopt a different dimension of ministry as their contribution to the effort. They are committed to evangelism, discipleship and church planting, and these commitments often place them at odds with the governments of countries where their target populations reside. Nevertheless, because nonresidential missionaries live outside their target areas, in free and open cities, they work in compliance with the laws of the land. While operating legally and openly from bases in world class cities, they must maintain a posture of discretion and sensitivity. They will often know the identities of agencies and individuals who have adopted ministry roles requiring a lower profile to maintain security.

A nonresidential missionary is not merely a researcher. While research is extremely important as a tool to better understand and minister to a population target, it is always a means to an end and never an end in itself. The goal remains firmly anchored in the Great Commission: "teaching them to observe whatsoever things I have commanded you; baptizing them in the name of the Father and of the Son and of the Holy Ghost."

As can be seen both from the descriptive paragraphs and the corrective disclaimers, a nonresidential missionary is a frontier evangelist committed to the use of every God-given means possible to present the gospel to the unevangelized world.

## THREE

Genesis of a new strategy

THE SEEMINGLY SUDDEN DEVELOPMENT and rapid expansion of nonresidential missions have led many to ask where the concept originated.
The term "nonresidential missionary" was first coined in 1986 by a
team of mission researchers working at the Southern Baptist Foreign
Mission Board in Richmond, Virginia. The concept of nonresidential
missions grew out of research associated with the *World Christian
Encyclopedia*, which revealed in an unprecedented fashion the enormous extent of the world's Christian resources and the paradoxical
existence of 1.3 billion unevangelized persons.[1]

Out of this new body of research emerged a growing awareness
of both the problems and possibilities associated with completing the
task of world evangelization. It was the range of possibilities that most
intrigued the researchers. These possibilities came to be encapsulated
in the concept of the nonresidential missionary.

Though the term, *nonresidential missionary*, was coined in Richmond, those who adopted it are quick to admit that the concept was
largely a product of its time. Says David Barrett, editor of the *World
Christian Encyclopedia*, "The development of nonresidential mission is
the inevitable result of the current world situation. It is somewhat like
the invention of the optical telescope in 1608 which was developed
simultaneously by a half-dozen individuals all working independently
of one another. In that situation, the art of lens grinding had just
reached a new level of proficiency and the public interest in the science
of astronomy was at an all-time high. The convergence of the two
factors led inevitably to the invention of the optical telescope." To put
it another way, it was an invention whose time had come.

In the same way, nonresidential missions is an idea whose time
has come—and accordingly it is being developed under various names

---

1   David B. Barrett, ed., *World Christian Encyclopedia* (New York: Oxford
     University Press, 1982).

and emphases all over the world. As the end result of a confluence of factors, it occurs wherever certain elements are at play: a) a high level of Christian commitment to fulfill the Great Commission; b) an unprecedented climate for cooperative efforts between Christians; c) the challenge of highly restricted countries and cities which forbid traditional missionary residence; and d) new breakthroughs in information, telecommunications and transportation technologies.

Commitment to the task

Though the Great Commission has been at the heart of the Christian missionary movement for nearly two millennia, it is difficult to find a time when its completion has been so visibly within the grasp of the church. This is largely because for the first time in history, research capabilities have brought the task into focus, enabling us to fully appreciate the enormity of the task and the remarkable progress that has already been made.

While there are more Christians in the world today than at any time in previous history, research now reveals an intractable 1.3 billion individuals who have yet to hear the Gospel message. In generations past, we might have been excused from this neglect by sheer ignorance. But today's global village includes decadal censuses of all the world's countries, revealing precisely where Christianity has penetrated and where it has yet to go.

Climate of cooperation

Fortunately, this same global village has also led the world's diverse Christian communities to discover and embrace one another as we work side by side. Much credit for this is due to the galvanizing effect of the closing second millennium. As mission agencies the world over develop global evangelization plans, they have inevitably discovered overlapping interests and aims. Although with 23,500 separate denominations, the diversity of the world's Christian communions is staggering, the opportunities for cooperation in the unfinished task have never been greater.

Another exciting development is the emergence of a missions-minded Two-Thirds World church. News of Jesus Christ is no longer going just from North to South, but also from churches in Asia, Africa, and Latin America to people all over the world. The possibilities of partnership and shared expertise are just beginning to be explored, as Christians of every nation work side by side to obey Christ's mandate.

New barriers in a changing world

From the point of view of Christian mission, one of the most challenging geopolitical developments of the post-World War II era has been the dramatic collapse of the old Western colonial empires and the subsequent emergence of autonomous nations. In the decades immediately following the end of World War II, we witnessed the most astonishing contraction of political empires that has ever been seen in so short a time. During the post-war era, lesser wars of independence erupted throughout the globe. In the single year of 1960, 18 new nations achieved independence.

Wars of independence led to wars of secession and boundary disputes around the globe, pitting tribal, religious and economically disparate groups against one another in the struggle for the future of their new nations. Each new conflict further destabilized the prospects for foreign missions as it effectively redrew our map of the world.

For traditional missionaries, these global birth pangs have had dire consequences. The new wave of nationalism often exhibited its first fruits in the expulsion, persecution or severe restriction of Western missionaries. China was the most extreme example, but parallels of lesser magnitude took place from Cuba to Burma, Vietnam to Sudan. In each case, the tragedy was not so much that people were locked out of these nations but that people were locked in—isolated from the gospel of Jesus Christ.

As of 1988, 45 countries in the world could be categorized as highly inaccessible to Christian witness or traditional missionary presence. Within these 45 nations live more than 2.6 billion persons, half of whom have never been given an opportunity to respond to the good news of Jesus Christ. Adding to the bleakness of this picture is the fact that from the end of World War II to the present time, countries have closed down or severely restricted missionary work at a rate of about three countries per year.

Today, almost one-fourth of the world's population has never been exposed to the gospel. These people have remained locked behind inaccessible national boundaries for much of this century. Despite *glasnost* and *perestroika*, global trends promise little hope of a reversal for traditional mission efforts. Due to the escalating birth rate in many of these countries, and the increasing number of country closures, the outlook for bringing the gospel to the whole world through traditional methods is discouraging.

New tools and resources

While prospects for the unevangelized world appear rather dismal, an assessment of the parts of the world where people have had a chance to hear and respond to the gospel is quite different. Christianity (in the broadest sense of the term) now accounts for more than 1.7 billion people—almost one-third of the world's population. Resources available to the worldwide church are staggering. Though Christians account for less than one-third of the world's population, we control 62% of the world's wealth with an annual aggregate income of $8.9 trillion. Christians give more than $8.6 billion to nearly 4,000 foreign mission-sending agencies, which sponsor hospitals, schools, churches, seminaries and more than 285,000 missionaries throughout the world. These Christians currently possess and use the lion's share of all the world's modern resources: airplanes, telephones, printing presses, computers, automobiles, and televisions.[2]

Since the end of World War II, missionaries have demonstrated considerable imagination in applying the gospel to a world growing ever more complex. Methods and approaches to ministry have included translation work, literacy missions, aviation fellowships, radio and television, discipleship, mass and personal evangelism, publishing, "tentmaking" methods, relief work, "gospel ships," and more. These various missionary approaches have been accompanied by ministries focusing on particular segments of society including Muslims, Jews, athletes, children, tribal peoples, Soviets, Arabs, businessmen, seamen, and so forth.

Imagine 23,500 denominations, each commissioned by Christ to go and make disciples of all the nations. Imagine 285,000 Christian cross-cultural missionaries and more than 4,000 cross-cultural mission agencies. Imagine 1.7 billion Christians commissioned by Christ to share the good news with those in need of it. For the nonresidential missionary, these resources form nothing less than an assortment of tools prepared by God for use in the fulfillment of his Great Commission.

But is it biblical?

The nonresidential mission may look like the appropriate missionary strategy for the twenty-first century, but is it consistent with the first century mission work we learn about in the Bible? Reliance upon computers, telecommunications systems and elaborate plans invariably prompts us to ask: "What does the Bible have to say about this?"

A survey of any concordance reveals that the term "nonresidential" does not appear in the Bible. But then, neither does the word "missionary"! Is it enough then to conclude that the nonresidential missionary idea is unbiblical? BY NO MEANS!

Many things which we take for granted in modern Christian missions lack direct scriptural sanction. What mission agency has not depended at some time on the assistance of Mission Aviation Fellow-

---

2   David B. Barrett, "The World in Statistics," *International Bulletin of Missionary Research,* January 1990.

ship, an organization dedicated to piloting missionaries into remote geographical regions? It would be difficult to find a Bible translation project today that is not dependent on state-of-the-art computer technology and "cutting-edge" linguistics software. Likewise, the advent of radio broadcasting has made the gospel available to millions of people in countries around the world who would otherwise never know of Christ's love for them. Yet each of these key resources—"airplanes," "computers," and "radio"—is noticeably absent from the pages of Scripture.

What clearly is mandated within the Bible is the commission to take the gospel of Jesus Christ to the ends of the earth, to every people, tongue and tribe. To achieve this goal, early Christians used every resource at their disposal. Today's nonresidential missionary stands in a long tradition of entrepreneurial missionaries determined to submit every means at their disposal to the Lordship of Christ, in the service of his Great Commission.

To better understand the scriptural warrant for a nonresidential ministry, let us look at four of the key elements in a nonresidential ministry: 1. Focus on unreached peoples; 2. Penetrating restricted access countries; 3. Devising a comprehensive and multi-faceted evangelism strategy; and 4. Assuming nonresidence for purposes of working through others.

Every tribe and tongue

From the earliest pages of the Bible, God has revealed his will that all the peoples of the world should experience the blessings of salvation. In the Abrahamic covenant as recorded in Genesis 22:18, God promises that all the nations of the earth are to be blessed through Abraham's seed.

In the words of the psalmist, God is not satisfied that only Israel know and praise him. The psalmist looks with longing to a time when "Thy way may be known upon earth, Thy saving health among all nations... O God, let all the people praise thee....and all the ends of the earth shall fear him" (Psalm 67).

It was out of love for the whole world that God sent his son as its savior (John 3:16). In his closing instructions to his disciples, Jesus pointed them to the ends of the earth with the command that disciples be made of all nations (Matthew 28:20; Acts 1:8). And when he was asked when the end times would come, he linked them to the fulfillment of his mandate to take the gospel to every nation (Matthew 24:14).

Paul was consumed by Christ's call to the frontiers. In his letter to the Romans, he revealed the heart of his missionary impetus: "I have strived to preach the gospel, not where Christ was named lest I should build upon another man's foundation: But as it is written, To whom he was not spoken of, they shall see: and they that have not heard shall understand" (Romans 15:20-21).

Finally, in an eschatological glimpse through the eyes of John of the Apocalypse, we read of the Great Commission's ultimate fulfillment: "After this I beheld, and lo, a great multitude, which no man could number, of all nations and kindreds, and people, and tongues, stood before the throne, and before the Lamb, clothed with white robes and palms in their hands; And cried with a loud voice saying, Salvation to our God which sitteth upon the throne, and unto the Lamb" (Revelation 7:9ff). The prophets foretold it; Jesus commanded it; and the Book of Revelation assures us that it will come to pass.

A history of barriers

The term "restricted access countries" refers to those countries in which it is either illegal or dangerous to proclaim the gospel message. One reason the notion of taking the gospel into restricted access countries is so troublesome to modern-day Christians is the legacy of 16th- to 19th-century missions. Missions during these centuries were plagued with many hardships, but rarely faced restrictions from non-Christian nations without having the muscle of some Western political power behind them. When missionaries were threatened in the Americas, Spanish and Portuguese armadas rushed to their defense. The same armed support ensured the accessibility of mission fields from North Africa to Indonesia, and from southern Africa to Manchuria.

This three-century legacy of Western muscle in Christian missions has led many 20th-century Christians to assume it as their inalienable right to have unlimited access to foreign lands. At the same time, we are quick to support the deportation from our own country of "effective" though radical missionaries such as the Bhagwan Sri Rajneesh or the Rev. Sun Myung Moon.

Though a guarantee of missionary residence could be assumed in the 19th century, a broader view of the history of Christian missions reveals that this is not the norm. Even though missionary activity was illegal throughout most of the world during the first four centuries, Christians continued to obey the Great Commission. Even after Constantine's ascension to the imperial throne in the fourth century, Christian missions continued to press into restricted access countries from Persia to Siam for the next thousand years. These bold forays into restricted regions followed a biblical model replete with examples.

One of the earliest episodes of God's delivering a closed population into the hands of his people was the conquest of Jericho, a city "shut up tight...none went out, and none came in" (Joshua 6:1). Of this impenetrable city, God declared: "See, I have given it unto thine hand" (Joshua 6:2). No restricted population target is closed to the power of

God. When his servants are obedient and resourceful, they are invited to participate in his mission to these difficult places.

Through the agency of the Holy Spirit and the conversion of an Ethiopian eunuch, the Lord enabled Philip to penetrate the restricted lands of sub-Saharan Africa with the gospel message (Acts 8:26ff). Bible scholars tell us that the Ethiopian eunuch was likely from the Cushitic kingdom of Meroe on the Nile River south of Egypt. Meroe was outside the bounds of the Roman empire and was closed to any sort of missionary incursions during the first century.

Similarly, the city of Damascus under the rule of King Aretus was hostile to missionary penetration. Overcoming considerable opposition, Paul managed to preach to its inhabitants until he was forced to escape through an unguarded window and a convenient basket (2 Corinthians 11:23ff).

From the time that Christianity was severed from the legal Jewish faith—A.D. 70 at the latest—Christianity was an illicit religion, and its missionary proclamation an illegal act. Today, Christian missionaries find themselves having come full circle. Once again they face a world not unlike that which awaited Jesus and his disciples: a world in which gospel proclamation is expressly forbidden. The question remains whether Christians of the 20th century will rise to the challenge in a manner consistent with that of their first century forebears.

Comprehensive strategies in the Bible

The Old Testament is full of accounts of comprehensive and multi-faceted plans aimed at the accomplishment of great feats. Noah's design and construction of an ark was God's means of saving not only a remnant people, but an entire cross section of the world's fauna. Joseph's mastery of an intricate famine survival plan ensured both his success and the continued existence of God's people in the second millennium before Christ. Moses led a remarkable relocation of the entire nation of Israel through obedience to God and careful planning. His successor, Joshua, worked out a plan of attacking the great cities of Palestine before beginning a mopping-up operation in Canaan. King David laid out an elaborate plan for building the temple and spent much of his life stockpiling supplies for its construction. Ezekiel revealed the same meticulous attention to detailed planning in his visions of the new temple described in chapters 40 - 43 of his book.

In the New Testament, Jesus' mission and ministry are characterized by careful planning as well as by the use of diverse methods. Following his Galilean ministry, Jesus resolutely "set his face toward Jerusalem" and began moving toward the conclusion of his predetermined course. Jesus advised his followers to take inventory of the task before them and plan for its completion. In Luke 14:28f, he said: "Which of you, intending to build a tower, sitteth not down first, and counteth the cost, whether he have sufficient to finish it? Lest haply, after he hath laid the foundation, and is not able to finish it, all that behold it begin to mock him."

Is it non-incarnational?

One of the most troublesome aspects of the nonresidential missionary approach for many is its apparent detachment from direct "incarnational" involvement. This is largely a result of the history of personal missionary involvement in direct witness; the biblical imperative to *go* to the ends of the earth; and the modern spirit of activism. Ironically, most of the places that merit the title "ends of the earth" strictly forbid residential, incarnational missionary presence. Consequently, tens of thousands of residential missionaries in ever-increasing numbers congregate in "open" countries, while untouched lands remain untouched. In short, if the ends of the earth are to be assailed, then nonresidential ministry that equips others and capitalizes on their gifts must be taken seriously.

Every sizeable undertaking recorded in the Bible involved the use of co-workers and the delegation of responsibility to them for its completion. Moses quickly realized the necessity of organizing the twelve tribes into administrative and fighting units, each with its own responsibilities for successfully completing the exodus and eventually settling into the land of Canaan. Nowhere is Moses's "nonresidential" commitment to working through others more vividly seen than at Rephidim, where he delegated leadership of Israel's armies against the Amalekites to Joshua, while maintaining a vigilant watch over the battle from the vantage point of a hilltop (Exodus 17:9-14). Every king of Israel relied upon a similar military and administrative chain of command to direct his efforts. The task at hand was simply too vast to undertake without a host of co-laborers.

In the New Testament, Jesus began his ministry with the selection of twelve disciples, symbolic of the twelve tribes of Israel, thus creating a new Israel and affirming the need to delegate his work through the participation of others. It is no coincidence that both Jesus and Paul made it their practice not to baptize new believers (John 4:2; 1 Corinthians 1:16f). They knew that others would have to assume this responsibility, since the fulfillment of their particular ministries required them to move on.

It was never the intention of Jesus or Paul that only one method of proclamation be pursued. In his most enduring metaphor for the church, "the body of Christ," Paul highlighted the need for diversity as well as unity (Romans 12:4ff). Missionaries today—residential and nonresidential alike—recognize the need for diversity and unity in crafting a comprehensive strategy. The only difference is whether the strategy is implemented from within or without the targeted location.

During his brief three-year ministry on earth, Jesus represented God's deepest endorsement of an incarnational witness to the world. Following this model, missionaries through the ages have obediently sought to incarnate the gospel to a dying world. The missionary model of Jesus' life does not end with the incarnation, however. After his ascension and resurrection, Christ assured his disciples that even greater things would be done through them. By multiplying his ministry in and through the lives of his disciples, Jesus taught the value of working through and with others to fulfill the Great Commission. The twin lessons of incarnation and multiplication of ministry can both be derived from the example of Jesus Christ.

## FOUR

Two mountaintop experiences

LENA RABANG HAS JUST SPENT THE PAST TWO DAYS trekking into the Sarawak highlands to reach the Mendalang Muslims in Indonesia. Before becoming a nonresidential missionary, Lena spent ten years as a dedicated Bible woman—a special category of service reserved for women from the Philippines who work as full-time, Christian evangelists, lay pastors and Bible teachers to the unreached tribes of the Philippines.[1]

Lena's ten years serving the Negritos of the Visayan Islands prepared her well for her work as a nonresidential missionary to the Mendalang. She learned the value of patience, the necessity of courage and the importance of careful planning in order to incorporate church planting and discipleship training to complement personal evangelism. After ten years, she had seen 47 churches planted among the Visayan Negritos and an equal number of lay pastors trained to lead the churches in continued growth and witness.

It was at this juncture in her Negrito ministry, three years ago, that Lena began to pray for the Muslims of Indonesia. As she studied more about them, she began to focus in on the Mendalang people. Not only were they ethnically Malay—like herself—they were a rare instance of a matrilineal and in some ways matriarchal community (one where women hold a high degree of authority and retain property rights) ensconced in a patriarchal religion—Islam. Missionaries who had tried to reach the Mendalang had invariably fallen short of their goal, either by failing to reach the women of the society, or by evoking the machismo ire of the male population. Consequently, the earliest missionaries were martyred among the Mendalang, and since that time other missionaries had been discouraged from approaching them.

---

1   The nonresidential ministries described in this chapter have actually taken place somewhere in the unevangelized world. Identities, population target and details have all been altered to protect those involved.

It is difficult for Lena to give the reason, but gradually she began to sense that God was drawing her to make a deeper commitment to reach the Mendalang. For nearly a year, she and her Negrito and Filipino brothers and sisters prayed for the Mendalang people and sought God's guidance about how to reach them. Missionary visas were not being granted to Filipino Christians at the time, and even if they were, none would be allowed to set up an overt mission to the Mendalang. It was then that Lena learned about the nonresidential approach.

Once she had settled on a nonresidential approach to the Mendalang, Lena quickly discovered that she could easily obtain a six-month visa. With the assistance of rotating co-workers, she was soon able to establish a steady presence of four other Filipino Bible women working in Mendalang at any given time.

Their Malay features eliminate most ethnic barriers in sharing the gospel. The fact that they are women gives them direct and immediate access to the women of Mendalang, while disarming any sense of threat to the men. Their faith is not characterized by many of those things which the Mendalang Muslims have historically found so offensive. They have no place for graven images in their worship; they are in the most literal sense "a people of the Book;" their personal morals are as conservative as their Muslim counterparts as they avoid alcohol and tobacco. Consequently, Lena's itinerant team of Filipino Bible women has seen remarkable openness among the Mendalang people. Three Bible study groups have already been organized, consisting of thirty sincere "seekers."

By next year, Lena knows that she must completely turn over her ministry of itinerant evangelism among the Mendalang to her Filipino co-workers. As a nonresidential missionary, there are too many other urgent projects demanding her attention—projects that can only be tended from a base outside the restrictions of Sumatra.

For more than a year, Lena has been lobbying the offices of SEABC (South East Asia Broadcasting Company) to begin a gospel radio broadcast in the Mendalang language. In order to ensure the project, she must dedicate more of her time to providing their offices in Manila with the resource material they will need. She is also anxious to begin the arduous task of resurrecting an old Mendalang Bible translation published by Dutch missioners in the 19th century. The translation is now out of print, but even if it were not, it would still require extensive reworking. For all of their good work, these early Dutch missioners had little idea about how to contextualize Scripture to the cultures and values of an Indonesian Muslim society. As a result, much that appears in the old translation is offensive to the Mendalang.

Of course, Lena will not be able to do the re-translation herself; that is a job for experts. Her task is typical of the nonresidential missionary: advocating this crucial need before those Christian experts, whether she finds them in Manila, Amsterdam or New York.

Lena is patient, but she is also tenacious. Whatever it takes to see the Mendalang mountain people—her people—respond to the good news of Christ, she is prepared to do it...or see to it that it is done.

Another mountaintop

Outside, the snow is beginning to accumulate on the Alpine slopes overlooking the foggy city of Salzburg, Austria. Eight nonresidential missionary couples are meeting around the fireplace in the common room of a rustic mountain hostel converted from a 17th-century Catholic convent.

From the exposed oaken beams of the vaulted ceiling above them, great sculpted angels and medieval saints peer down at the intense interaction below. The bustling activity taking place is the annual team-cluster meeting of nonresidential missionaries convened from all over the world. Heavy on their agenda is the review of one another's priority goals and action plans—the flesh and bones of their comprehensive strategy to serve their people.

The table top is strewn with notepads, "people profiles," and a half-dozen humming lap-top computers. Conversation is intense, as each nonresidential missionary carefully combs over the presenter's master plan.

"I really do not know what to do with these United Bible Societies people," Sean says. "I must have written or called them a hundred times. It is as if they have no desire to see a Kimchak Bible translation!"

"Hey, don't get all bent out of shape — I mean, don't be so anxious, Sean," says Sonia, quickly translating her American slang as she catches the puzzled frowns on the faces of her multi-national colleagues. "There are reasons for their cold reception to the idea of a Kimchak Bible."

"That's right," adds her husband, Brian. "In the 1920s, they were faced with the opportunity of translating a Turkish Bible with the full blessings of the government. It seems the government of Turkey even agreed to allow the book to be openly distributed in local bookstores, but one stipulation was made: the United Bible Societies must never participate in the translation of any minority language Scriptures."

"They felt it would aggravate their already ethnically divided country," says Sonia.

"Well, it is helpful to know a little of the history behind this problem," replies Sean. "But what do I do now?"

"Well, what are your options?" asks Rita. "Remember, the principle of multi-processing! There's always more than one way to get something done."

"I have had great response from the International Bible Translators in Stockholm," Anna says. "Here is their business card."

"Better yet," Ian adds, "I seem to recall that there's a Wycliffe team of Bible translators who are just finishing their ten-year project on the Sorani Bible. They just might have someone free enough to consider taking on a new project."

"That would be perfect," Sean replies, smiling. "The Sorani and Kimchak languages are linguistically very close. Someone with experience in Sorani would be an ideal match. I will pursue this right away."

Michael, the "eldest" of the nonresidential missionaries, with three years of nonresidential ministry under his belt, takes charge. "Okay folks, it's time for us to move on and help Juan and Elena sharpen their goals and action plans for reaching the Gandahli of Nepal. Who wants to go first? All right, Emil and Maria."

Maria begins, "Juan and Elena, I want to commend you. Your prayer base looks really strong. Three hundred praying churches is a formidable spiritual army!"

Emil adds, "I have to agree, but I have some questions about your goals and actions related to Christian presence among the Gandahli. I know you are confirmed Brazilian Baptists, but I think you are relying a bit too heavily on your own denomination's resources to reach the Gandahli when more appropriate and more extensive personnel resources are being overlooked."

"Maybe you're right," Juan says. "I admit I'm a bit deficient in my understanding of some of the Two-Thirds World resources in Asia. What do you recommend, John?"

John and his wife Anna are evangelical Christians from Trivandrum, India. "Indian Christians should be your greatest resource for establishing a witnessing presence in Nepal, my friend," he says. "Not only are geographical proximity and smooth visa access in your favor, but most Indian Christians also share close ethnic affinity with the Gandahli. This makes it easier for them to cross over cultural barriers to share their faith. As far as resources are concerned, there are so many in India. In Madras alone you have the IMA, or India Missions Association, the Church Growth Research Centre, Union Seminary, the Friends Missionary Prayer Band and many, many more."

"I'm beginning to get the picture," Juan says as he hurriedly scribbles names and places onto his notepad. "I think I'm going to need to plan a trip next month to your country!"

"Before you come," Anna says, "let us help you draw up a list. Most of the people you will want to talk with may be reached by fax or telephone first. These advance contacts will make your visits much more fruitful. Then, when you come, do plan to stay with us!"

The conversation and interaction persist well into the night and will continue for three more days. At the end of their time together, each nonresidential missionary will have sharper, more detailed goals and action plans. Then each set of plans will be offered once again to the Lord in a dedication service scheduled for the final night of the meeting. As they leave the mountaintop, these nonresidential missionaries will renew their commitment to serve people they hope will respond to the love of Christ.

## FIVE

Why so many have never heard

HOW IS IT THAT A CHURCH SO RICH in resources can continue, year in and year out, to live side by side with 1.3 billion people isolated from the love of Christ? "It isn't for want of trying that the world remains unevangelized," some would argue. Hundreds of thousands of missionaries have gone out over the years to their respective "Jerusalems, Judeas, Samarias and ends of the earth." Along the way they endured enormous hardship, and the history of Christian mission is a history of martyrdom. But despite extreme sacrifice, many regions remained untouched by the gospel. Today, the nearly 300,000 foreign missionaries deployed would appear to be more than adequate to the task, and yet the plight of these regions persists.

Numerous reasons have been given to explain why they have not been able to hear and respond to the gospel. Among the most commonly raised are: 1) socio-cultural barriers, 2) geographical & political barriers, 3) a fragmented Christian world, and 4) the convenience factor. The nonresidential missionary may provide the extra momentum needed to push the Church past some or all of these barriers.

Bridging socio-cultural gaps

A good example of an enduring socio-cultural challenge is found among the nomadic peoples of the world. Migrant throughout their history, these largely pastoral peoples are constantly in pursuit of seasonal water or pastures, or retreating from the ravages of the desert or mountain cold. Typically, nomadic peoples vary their residence between winter and summer or wet and dry seasons.

For the traditional missionary family, the task of pursuing these peoples across some of the earth's most inhospitable terrain is simply impractical. For a nonresidential missionary, however, serving the nomads may be more feasible.

The first step is to identify the various points at which the people are resident. Through research, the nonresidential missionary is able to determine where the peoples spend the dry season; where they go during the rains; the location of their market places; and what oases they frequent. To bridge the gaps between these points of residence, the nonresidential missionary might determine what type of radio broadcasts would most effectively reach these people while they are on the move.

The nonresidential missionary can identify pressing humanitarian needs facing the people. Would they welcome the help of a veterinarian or a medical doctor during the two months they are in a winter residence? Could they benefit from hydrologists providing wells at one of their meeting points?

The nonresidential missionary would also try to determine which nationalities and ethnic groups might provide the most appropriate and effective witness to the nomads. Then, through a comprehensive strategy that includes every possible resource, the nonresidential missionary could weave together a concerted effort to serve nomads in a manner that will result in viable, culturally-suited churches.

Overcoming geographical and political barriers

The problems associated with geographical and political barriers are similar to those of a socio-cultural nature. It is a tragedy of history that because most of the world's missionaries emanate from the Western bloc of nations, the countries with access to the gospel are those which are on amicable political terms with the West; and those with limited or no access to Christian witness are those which are politically at odds with the West.

In practical terms, this means traditional missionaries are shut out of countries which are hostile to Western presence. Such is the plight of Afghanistan, Mongolia, Iran—and the list goes on and on.

In the face of this challenge, nonresidential missionaries have acknowledged the need to be *global* mission strategists. Recognizing that Christ has followers in almost every country on earth, they look for people from nations and ethnic groups who—both culturally and politically—are better able to serve people in countries off-limits to citizens of the West.

Consequently, the most delightful of partnerships have unfolded. Indian Christians have set up businesses in Soviet Central Asia; Latin American Christians have done the same in Muslim North Africa. Nigerian and Zambian believers have taken the role of students to China and the USSR. Filipino domestic workers have carried their faith into the households of the wealthy oil barons of the Persian Gulf.

For the nonresidential missionary, geographical and political barriers dissolve in a pool of global Christian resources. This is because he starts at a fundamentally different point than a traditional residential missionary. The residential missionary must begin with the question: "What can *I* do to reach this people?" If legal residence is not a possibility, the geographical and political barrier immediately answers this question with a resounding, "Nothing."

The nonresidential missionary, on the other hand, begins with a different question: "What will it take to reach these people?" The answers that emerge are diverse and complex—but no more so than the resources available and the strategies that can be devised to meet the challenge.

Uniting a fragmented Christian world

Since the 19th century, a growing number of Christians have come to realize that the embarrassing state of a divided Christian world with its conflicting, competing and wastefully re-duplicated efforts has contributed much to the fact that so many have never responded to the gospel. With more than 23,000 Christian denominations worldwide the problem of a fragmented Christianity is not likely to go away soon. This should not mean the worst elements of fragmentation have to be tolerated.

For nonresidential missionaries, the diversity of the Church provides a pool of resources that must be coordinated to maximum benefit by eliminating the problems associated with competition, redundancy and waste.

It is important that the notion of matching a nonresidential missionary to a single unevangelized population not be confused with the old "comity" arrangements which were attempted in the early decades of this century. Through comity agreements, mission agencies and denominations essentially divided up the world into ecclesiastical fiefdoms, being careful, for example, not to interject Baptist witness into expressly Lutheran territory, and vice versa. The goal of minimizing proselytization and maximizing limited resources was laudatory, but when one denominational group failed to achieve its commitment to evangelize its designated assignment, the big losers, again and again, were the many individuals without any understanding about Jesus.

The nonresidential approach turns comity on its head. Not only does a nonresidential missionary assignment preclude a comity-type exclusivity, it actually requires the joint efforts of a range of mission-minded agencies and individuals.

David Barrett refers to this as the "kaleidoscopic approach to world evangelization." Each missionary contribution to the evangelization of a people—whether through prayer from 10,000 miles away or through indigenous efforts from within the heart of the unreached territory—is incomplete and insufficient when viewed in isolation. When it is seen from God's perspective, however, all of the ministries flow together into a divinely arranged configuration, like the random pieces of broken glass and colored gemstones sift into the beautifully ordered patterns of a kaleidoscopic image.

It is the job of the nonresidential missionary to see that the patterns harmonize, and that as little as possible is wasted. From the position of communicating with all the various people involved, the nonresidential missionary is able to foresee potential crisis points and eliminate unnecessary conflicts, redundancies or omissions. Drawing from the enormous resource pool of Christian resources and bathing them in prayer, the nonresidential missionary is in a privileged position to observe the Holy Spirit's multi-faceted redemptive work among a long-neglected or deeply entrenched people.

Battling the convenience factor

In his book, *Countdown to 1900*, Todd Johnson recalls an illustration used by Stanley Smith in the 19th century that highlights one of the most vivid and persistent reasons for the unfinished task. Smith identifies the inadequate distribution of a more than adequate gospel as the chief reason for the world's lack of evangelization, and lays the blame for this condition at the doorstep of the Christian world. Addressing a large assembly in London, Smith reminded his audience of the miracle of Jesus feeding the five thousand:

> Imagine the disciples are here distributing the food, and that this great assembly is the hungry multitude that is waiting to be fed. They go to the first row of benches distributing the food, and to the second, and the third, and the fourth, and so on to the eighth row. But at the end of the eighth row they stop and turn back to the first, and feed these eight rows again, pouring bread and fish into their laps and piling it about them, leaving the starving multitudes behind uncared for. What do you suppose our Lord would say if he were here? Let us take the parable to ourselves, for this is what we have been doing. We have been feeding these nearest to us over and over again with the bread which our Lord has given us, and have neglected the multitudes beyond.[1]

The truth of Smith's illustration must not be lost on the Christian world of our generation. It has never been more true than today. Research indicates that of every $100 spent by the Christian world on specifically Christian causes of missions, ministry and service, only one penny ever reaches the unevangelized world. Typically, Christians

---

1   Quoted in Todd M. Johnson's *Countdown to 1900*, (Birmingham, Alabama: New Hope, 1988).

continue to spend $99 dollars out of every $100 on ourselves—those whom Stanley Smith called "the first row of benches" simply because "these (are) nearest us." Viewing Smith's illustration from the perspective of the Lord who initiated the miraculous feeding, we cannot help but imagine how grieved he must be at the tragic disobedience of his servants.

Nonresidential missionaries are gospel "redistribution agents." They plead the case of their people before the world court of Christian conscience. If their people have no Scripture, the nonresidential missionary lobbies for this cause. If they are without the fundamental necessities of life, the nonresidential missionary seeks out those agencies and individuals who can provide them the basics of food, water and shelter, and in the process share a message of eternal life. As a tireless advocate on behalf of a people, the nonresidential missionary speaks for those without a voice in the world of Christian resources because they have no constituency there.

## SIX

Two families at work

A TELEPHONE RINGS IN A MODESTLY FURNISHED ninth floor flat in Hong Kong's New Territories. Though no one is home, an answering machine assumes responsibility for accepting the call: "You have reached the *Apang Advocate*. We are away from the telephone right now. Please leave your name, number and a short message and we will get back with you (beep)."

Two hours later, eighteen-year-old Jonathan Kowles places a long-distance telephone call from Singapore to the same Hong Kong telephone number.[1] After the answering machine begins to recite its familiar litany, Jonathan places his portable "code-a-phone" over the telephone mouthpiece and enters a three-digit code. The Hong Kong answering machine responds to his command by playing back the three messages he has received that day.

The first call is from a local Chinese pastor: "I have some letters for the believers in Apang Province. Do you know when the next courier will be going in?" The second is from an inquirer wishing to be added to the circulation list for the monthly *Apang Advocate* newsletter.

The third message is unusual and immediately summons Jonathan's full attention: the message is spoken in the rural Apang language. A young Apang voice nervously continues: "My name is Liu-man. I just arrived in Hong Kong by fishing boat from the mainland. Pastor Wei said you could help me find some fellow Christians. I am staying at the Shang-ti Guest House in Ho Man Tin. Please come and see me."

Jonathan glances at his calendar watch. The conference he is attending on unevangelized peoples of Asia will continue for another couple of days. But it is five in the afternoon in Taipei, Taiwan, where

---

1   The nonresidential ministries described in this chapter have actually taken place somewhere in the unevangelized world. Identities, population target and details have all been altered to protect those involved.

his nonresidential missionary parents are visiting Jonathan's grand-parents. Jonathan picks up the phone again and dials the number.

Jonathan's grandparents, Wilfred and Rebecca Kowles, came to Asia as missionaries in 1926. They had only been married a year and both were under the age of twenty-five when they reached the Himalayan foothills along the border of what is now China and Burma. They settled there among a tribal people of nearly eight hundred thousand Tibeto-Burmese villagers who called themselves the Apang.

Over the next twenty years, they served the Apang, taking steps in the journey of making Christ known to the people. Although most of their missionary colleagues fled the country during the Second World War, the Kowles family remained. Sequestered in their mountain village, they felt sheltered from much of the chaos enveloping the rest of the world.

The war years proved to be the most fruitful for the Apang work. During the eight years from 1940 to 1948, the Kowleses saw nearly a thousand Apang come to know Christ. Mr. Kowles organized the new believers into churches, and began training his first class of ten Apang pastors to lead the fledgling churches.

The year 1948 was a significant one for Wilfred and Rebecca. It was the year that their son, Jonathan's father Robert, was born, and also the year that Maoist Communism first penetrated the villages of Apang province. Foreigners increasingly came under scrutiny as agents of colonialism and imperialism. For the Kowleses, this was a difficult period.

By 1949, most of China had fallen to the Communists. Although Apang Province held out for another two years, it was becoming more and more difficult for the Kowleses to remain there. Finally, on Christmas Eve, 1949, Wilfred bade his wife and children good-bye. Placing them on a river boat that would take them to the coast, he remained behind to face whatever might unfold.

Six months later, he was arrested, interrogated and imprisoned. For four months, Kowles languished in an Apang prison, not knowing if he would ever be released. Only after repeated protests and solicitations from his wife and the American ambassador in Hong Kong, was Kowles finally released, and ordered never again to set foot in China.

The Kowles family went through years of denial that their fruitful ministry in China was over. Throughout the remainder of the decade of the fifties, they waited hopefully for China to reopen. With the advent of the Cultural Revolution in the mid-sixties, however, they realized that their hopes were unfounded. Wilfred and Rebecca settled into a less than satisfying ministry to Chinese refugees in Hong Kong.

By the early seventies, their son Robert had returned from America with his new bride, Julia. Robert joined his parents in their work, but soon found himself exploring the burgeoning network of underground ministry to the Chinese mainland. Wary of participating in what were explicitly illegal activities, Robert nevertheless prayed for these Christian risk-takers who were busily at work smuggling Christian Scriptures and literature into China wherever they could find an entry point.

By 1980, China was again showing signs of opening up—though with continued tight restrictions on foreign missionary presence. China desired Western business investment and access to global capitalist markets. This rush into the global marketplace meant China would have to acquire the emerging international language of trade— English. By 1983, an appeal for 14,000 English language teachers went out from the Beijing government. Suddenly, after decades of frustration, the Kowles family found itself with more opportunities for ministry and witness than they could possibly fill.

It was at this crucial juncture that Robert first picked up a copy of *700 Plans to Evangelize the World.*[2] In the chapters on nonresidential mission, Robert Kowles discovered what he was already on the threshold of becoming. Within months, he had organized his extended family and their own pool of Christian resources into a computerized network aimed at reviving a ministry to the Apang people. As a family team, they sat down and drew up detailed plans for reaching the Apang, beginning with a concerted global prayer effort.

Since adopting the nonresidential approach to reaching the Apang, the family has entered its third generation of missionary commitment to the Apang. After nearly three decades of stagnation, they are again seeing the gospel rekindled among the Apang. They are hopeful that the task will be completed before a fourth generation of Kowleses is required.

Seoul-searching for the Kweiji

At 6:30 a.m., Ron and Esther Park emerge from a two-hour prayer meeting with twelve other members of their Korean Presbyterian Church. Prayer for the nations is a daily routine for the Parks, but on Wednesdays they are joined by their friends in a special day of prayer and fasting for the evangelization of the 4.3 million Kweiji people of China.

---

2   David Barrett and James Reapsome, *700 Plans to Evangelize the World*, (Birmingham, Alabama: New Hope, 1988).

The Kweiji are a tribal non-Chinese people living in the mountainous interior of China. Their relative isolation and distinctives of language and race have insulated them from the remarkable growth of Christianity among the Han Chinese. The Kweiji are one of the largest peoples in Asia with no missionaries, Scripture or church. Official Chinese publications describe the Kweiji as atheists, but pre-revolutionary anthropological studies indicate their religion to be a blend of animistic and shamanistic practices.

Ron and Esther began their nonresidential ministry to the Kweiji three years ago. Their vocation stemmed from a calling to prayer for the peoples of the world who have never heard the gospel. After praying for several weeks, the Parks sensed that God was leading them to go a step further. That Sunday in church, they made public their decision to give their lives in service to the Kweiji people.

Since that time, prayer has become the foundation and wellspring of their ministry. Flowing out of this wellspring—now involving 300 Korean and 50 other evangelical churches in four countries—is Scripture translation, radio broadcasts, dozens of presence ministries and a network of cassette and gospel recording distribution.

Perhaps the most innovative of the Parks's efforts to reach the Kweiji came early in their ministry. Ron and Esther's initial research into the Kweiji revealed that these people were historically noted for their skills in archery. The year was 1987, and everyone in Korea was preparing for the 1988 Seoul Olympics. Esther was the first to speculate whether or not some of the Kweiji would be represented in the Olympic national team coming from China. Further investigation confirmed her hopes—the archery team from the Peoples' Republic of China consisted almost entirely of Kweiji. As the Olympic season drew close, prayer began around the clock for an opportunity to share the gospel with these Kweiji archers. At the time, neither Ron nor Esther knew the Mandarin language, much less that of the Kweiji.

Undaunted, they sought out the assistance of some bilingual friends. Over the month-long period that the Chinese Olympic team was in Seoul, Ron counted twelve different times and six different persons who were able to share the gospel with each of the Kweiji archers. Though no decisions for Christ were recorded, three young Kweiji men and women returned to their remote village with gospel tracts and Chinese New Testaments from their first friendly encounter with Christians. The Parks never met the Kweiji archers, except in their prayers, where they continue to hold them before the throne of grace to the present day.

In March of this year, the government opened two new districts to outsiders in the province where the Kweiji live, making tourism possible for the first time. Responding to Esther's words of encouragement, a young woman in their prayer group has taken it on herself to mobilize the women of the Korean Presbyterian missionary societies to consider visiting the beautiful waterfalls and scenic mountain lakes of the Kweiji hill country. To make these visits most effective, she provides all who go with "Christian Tourist Resource Kits." Each kit contains two New Testaments in the Mandarin language and seven newly produced gospel tracts in the language of the Kweiji people. The kit also contains a brief prayer profile on the Kweiji written by Esther and produced on her computer with a simple desktop publishing program.

Using their Samsung computer with an internal 2400 baud modem for telecommunications, Ron and Esther have linked up a prayer and mobilization network of Christians in South Korea, Hong Kong, the United States and Canada—a network of people who are committed to respond instantly to needs for prayer or action to benefit the cause of Christ among the Kweiji.

A year ago, their prayers and action brought about the establishment of a rural medical clinic in the village of Liujang—a sprawling hamlet of nearly 100,000 Kweiji people. Though Ron could not gain permanent visas for missionaries to live in Liujang, he was able to work with a Han Chinese midwife in the village who regularly meets the steady stream of Korean and Cantonese doctors who rotate into the clinic for voluntary shifts of two weeks to a month at a time. Through their witness, hundreds of Kweiji people have already heard the gospel, and the medical needs of an entire region are being adequately addressed for the first time.

A young Kweiji woman named Siu-chan, who is a student at the local university, began helping at the clinic soon after it opened. Day after day, she observed the kind treatment of the Christian doctors and nurses and listened to their words of testimony, until finally she made the message her own. Volunteering to serve as an interpreter for the doctors and nurses, Siu-chan went beyond the efforts of the government-provided interpreter who merely communicated the words of symptoms, diagnosis and prescriptions. Siu-chan communicated words of hope and faith. The medical teams were amazed at the fervor with which she shared her new-found faith. In the evening, after the clinic had closed for the day, one of them asked her the source of motivation.

"All my life," she said, "I have been searching for something to fill an emptiness inside. Nothing I had heard or experienced before could fill this empty place. You people are different. You really love us. When you told me about Jesus—at first I didn't know. But then one night I invited him to come into my life. Since that time, there is no more emptiness. Jesus is what I've been waiting for all my life."

Siu-chan is now studying the Bible, and helping with the translation of key Scripture texts and concepts into the language of the Kweiji. Already she looks forward to the time when she can share her new faith with her family, who live in a remote district of the province off limits to foreign visitors.

Siu-chan is one more thread in a growing tapestry of Kweiji evangelization. As more like her come to know Christ, it will be easier for the nonresidential efforts of the Parks to be multiplied and used to maximum effectiveness on the inside. In the meantime, much more work remains to be done.

## SEVEN

Training for the task

A NONRESIDENTIAL MISSIONARY DOES NOT EMERGE full-grown from the day the idea first comes to mind. After receiving and accepting a divine calling to become a nonresidential missionary, careful training must follow to provide the preparation necessary to complete the task.

Several different types of nonresidential missionary training have developed in different contexts around the world. The shortest is a two-and-a-half week program involving a self-instruction manual. The lengthiest stretches for more than eight weeks and includes a week-long survey trip to a place where Christ is not known.

Fundamental to all nonresidential training programs are five key component parts. The first three occur in sequence:

1. Exploring the world of Christian resources;
2. Investigating the world of your population target; and
3. Bringing resources to serve the needs of the target population.

The other two key component parts are somewhat more mundane, and are scattered throughout the training program:

4. Computer and telecommunications training; and
5. Administrative and logistical preparation.

This chapter presents the outline of a four-and-a-half week training program currently used by an agency with a nonresidential missionary program. It is not the only way to conduct training, but is given to provide some insight into how one agency has addressed the unique challenges of this kind of missionary preparation.

Stocking the toolbox

The first three week-long segments build sequentially one upon the other. The first full week segment is given to investigating the world of Christian resources. This is an opportunity for the nonresidential missionary trainee's mind to be stretched to consider the range of possibilities available to serve a restricted access population. The trainee can then accumulate a host of vital resources before actually making contact with the population target.

The second full week is spent exploring the population target. The trainee is expected to initiate intensively what will be a life-long pursuit of developing expertise in this area. Attention should be given to the history, language and evangelization status of the population, with an eye toward identifying the unique needs and opportunities evoked by this particular assignment.

The third week-long segment concentrates on weaving together the vast resources which concerned Christians offer with the specific needs of the population target. This week begins rather broadly, with an exercise of brainstorming a list of 100 evangelization and ministry options. The trainee then focuses on the specific task of identifying the seven most crucial evangelization needs, and converting these into concrete goals and action plans.

The two shorter components of nonresidential missionary training are computer training and administrative matters. These generally take four to five days each, and are scattered throughout the four-and-a-half-week training program.

Before detailing the schedule of nonresidential missionary training, a few items of preparation should be stated.

Preparation for training

1. *Prayer.* A daily prayer discipline directed toward serving the missionary's population segment should be developed from the first day of training. The prayer commitment should begin modestly, in a manner commensurate with the trainee's own understanding of the segment, and then grow to include crucial dimensions of the segment's evangelization status, as well as the various other Christians discovered in the process—Christians who either are or could be a part of the ongoing process. This prayer exercise will not only prepare the population target for evangelistic engagement, but will also work to bind the heart of the trainee to the population target and to future co-workers.

2. *Evaluation.* The trainee should be part of an ongoing process of evaluation, examination and feedback. This weekly feedback process is designed to keep the trainee moving through frustrating sticking points, help broaden the scope of investigation, and identify and shore up weaknesses.

3. *Husband and wife training.* It is certainly not a prerequisite for a nonresidential missionary to be married. But if the nonresidential missionary is married, it is imperative that both spouses receive training. Otherwise, the task will suffer from lack of unified effort. If a couple is working as a team, the work will be doubly strengthened. And since much nonresidential

missionary work can be equally accomplished by either a man or woman, joint training ensures a fulfilling ministry for two, for life.

4. *Equipment and budget needs.* Each trainee is expected to have the following:

   a. A working budget for networking and research use of long distance telephones, correspondence, and database information retrieval;

   b. A laptop computer needed for portability in commuting to various research locations, workshops and seminars;

   c. Software needs: DOS (Disk Operating System), BITCOM (or a comparable telecommunications software package), WordPerfect (or a comparable word processing software package), AskSam (or a comparable database program).

INTRODUCTION AND OVERVIEW: A half-week session

1. **Overview of the nonresidential missionary training program**

   Objective: To introduce and overview the nonresidential missionary training program.

   Action Steps:

   a. Explain the purpose of the 4 1/2-week training schedule.

   b. Preview the schedule.

   c. Detail expectations for the trainee: meetings, reading assignments, tasks, etc.

   d. Present as fully as possible the ultimate goal of a functioning nonresidential missionary.

   e. Begin an evangelization log which will include research notes, resource findings, networking information and evangelization strategies.

2. **Equipping for a nonresidential mission**

   Objective: To introduce the trainee to the computer hardware and software tools needed to fulfill the varied requirements of this type of mission.

   Action Steps:

   a. Provide the trainee with a basic introduction to his personal computer and to the DOS software.

   b. Provide the trainee with a basic introduction to WordPerfect and AskSam software.

   c. Preview bibliography for trainee's research.

WEEK ONE: Investigating the world of resources

1. **Overview of evangelization resources**

   Objective: To overview the necessity of a comprehensive understanding of the numerous existing and potential evangelization resources.

   Action Steps:
   a. Introduce the subjects of networking and evangelizing resources.
   b. Explain the absolute necessity for the trainee to understand and interface with diverse resources in order to assemble a comprehensive strategy of evangelization.
   c. Sketch numerous networking scenarios in which a variety of resources contribute toward evangelizing efforts.

2. **Evangelization resource networks**

   Objective: To examine thoroughly the potential evangelizing networks which exist within the various Christian denominational, non-denominational, and secular resources.

   Action Steps:
   a. Present the networks, nuances and distinctives of national and indigenous evangelizing resources.
   b. Present the networks, nuances and distinctives of Catholic and Orthodox evangelizing resources.
   c. Present the networks, nuances and distinctives of the various Protestant resources for evangelization.
   d. Present the networks, nuances and distinctives of the various non-denominational resources.
   e. Present the networks, nuances and distinctives of the various secular resources for evangelization.

3. **Networking**

   Objective: To supply the trainee with several means of building networks and the opportunity to initiate a network.

   Action Steps:
   a. Explain the concept of "networking".
   b. Provide insights and strategies for involving appropriate organizations, agencies and individuals in the process of evangelizing the target population segment.
   c. Introduce the trainee to the various means of networking: form letters, World Evangelization Database, telephone contacts, electronic messaging, personal visits, etc.

    d. Allow the trainee to initiate a network, using telephone and correspondence facilities of the mission agency.

4. Getting to work

Objective: To provide the trainee with an opportunity to explore the evangelizing resources relevant to his population segment.

Action Steps:

    a. Allow the trainee time to delve into sourcebooks, manuals, handbooks, etc., in order to better understand the resource possibilities.

    b. Instruct the trainee to select and list the resources which could potentially affect the evangelization of his or her population segment.

    c. Initiate involvement in the various religious and secular evangelizing resources.

5. Progress analysis and redirection

Objective: To evaluate and discuss with the trainee his or her understanding of the concept of networking and progress in this area; and, if necessary, redirect networking options.

Action Steps:

    a. Listen to the trainee's understanding of resources and their potential for evangelizing a population segment.

    b. Check the progress of the trainee's exploration into the world of resources.

    c. Provide constructive criticism, encouragement, and praise.

    d. Redirect and expand, if necessary, the trainee's understanding and focus in the area of evangelization resources.

WEEK TWO: Investigating the unevangelized population target

1. Gathering research on a population segment

Objective: To provide the trainee with an understanding of the sources and the skills to do research on a population segment.

Action Steps:

    a. Introduce and overview research methods and resources as they relate to a population segment.

    b. Define the research expectations for the trainee.

    c. Teach the trainee how to complete a people profile.

2. **Sources**

Objective: To detail the various sources (historical, contemporary, periodical, reference, etc.) and databases (NEXUS, LEXUS, OCLC, RIO, WEDB, etc.) available for the trainee to do research on the population segment.

Action Steps:

a. Immerse the trainee in the research sources available.

b. Conduct a series of database searches on the trainee's target population.

c. Allow the agency time to review the database printouts on the target population.

3. **Getting to work**

Objective: To provide the trainee an opportunity to explore sources, make database searches, and apply research methods in order to investigate his population segment.

Action Steps:

a. Allow the trainee to do research on the various resources at the missions research center library and other research centers.

b. Initiate a thorough understanding of the trainee's target population.

4. **Computerized telecommunications**

Objective: Provide the trainee with training in the use of BITCOM software and EasyLink telecommunications.

Action Steps:

a. Introduce the trainee to BITCOM telecommunications software.

b. Teach the trainee how to interface the BITCOM software with the other database and word processing computer applications.

c. Teach the trainee how to utilize EasyLink telecommunications capabilities.

5. **Progress analysis and redirection**

Objective: Evaluate and discuss the trainee's progress in gathering research on the population segment and, if necessary, to redirect research and focus. This element should be conducted as a dialog between agency staff, the trainee, and others in the program.

Action Steps:

a. Explain the purpose of the weekly "Progress analysis and redirection" element in the training.

b. Listen to the trainee's understanding of the research process and purpose.

c. Check the progress of the trainee's research into his population segment.

d. Provide constructive criticism, encouragement, and praise.

e. Redirect, if necessary, the trainee's research focus, intent, or methods.

WEEK THREE: Developing a comprehensive strategy

1. Turning research into action

Objective: To teach the trainee how to turn the voluminous research he has compiled into concrete action plans.

Action Steps:

a. Complete a worksheet that will help identify potential openings for witness.

b. Briefly list 100 evangelization options available to serve the population target.

2. Goals and action plans

Objective: To train the trainee in developing goals and action plans for the evangelization of his population segment.

Action Steps:

a. Illustrate the reasons why goals and action plans are a necessary part of the trainee's evangelizing strategy.

b. Instruct the trainee, step by step, in the development of potential goals and action plans.

c. List the various factors (resources, time and personnel constraints, contacts, ministry options, etc.) which should contribute to the development of the trainee's goals and action plans.

d. Check the trainee's progress to insure that the goals and action plans are attainable, quantifiable, and dated.

3. Action plans work session

Objective: To provide the trainee with a time to develop goals and action plans.

Action Steps:

a. Allow the trainee time to formulate goals and action plans.

b. Instruct the trainee to draft as many plans as possible during this work session for discussion in the next session.

4. Progress analysis and redirection

Objective: To evaluate and discuss with the trainee progress in the development and use of databases and in the formulation of goals and action plans, and if necessary, redirect.

Action Steps:

a. Listen to the trainee's understanding of the need for security and confidentiality, the purpose and function of the databases, and the mechanics of developing goals and action plans.

b. Check the trainee's progress in networking, use of the databases, and development of goals and action plans.

c. Provide constructive criticism, encouragement, and praise.

d. Redirect, if necessary, the trainee's focus, intent, or skills.

5. Work time

Objective: To provide the trainee with an opportunity to refine goals and action plans, build networks, view the Global Evangelization Resources Video Tapes, etc.

WEEK FOUR: Administrative and logistical wrap-up

1. Security and confidentiality

Objective: To explain the necessity of confidentiality and the various ways of securing data.

Action Steps:

a. Provide the trainee with a rationale for security and confidentiality specifically related to his assignment.

b. Detail security procedures currently in operation.

c. Suggest numerous personal procedures which should be adopted by the nonresidential missionary in order to insure a confident and secure network.

d. Outline guidelines for news articles, deputations, newsletters, and other communiques.

e. Secure a confidentiality agreement from the trainee.

2. Reporting

Objective: To explain reporting procedures and forms.

Action Steps:

a. Explain why reporting is important to global evangelization efforts.

b. Introduce reporting forms to the trainee.

c. Clearly explain the procedures and expectations for reporting.

d. Instruct the trainee to report on current progress as a nonresidential missionary.

3. Administration

Objective: To acquaint the trainee with budgeting and work procedures.

Action Steps:

a. Outline the administrative scheme of the nonresidential missionary program.

b. Detail the areas of administration for which the nonresidential missionary has primary responsibility.

c. Explain how and when operating budget and capital requests are made.

d. Explain the bookkeeping procedure for the nonresidential missionary.

e. Describe the reporting procedure, expectations and content.

4. Relationship with other mission administrative offices.

Objective: To provide a time for related mission administrators and the trainee to discuss related matters of concern.

Action Steps:

a. Facilitate a relationship between the nonresidential missionary trainee and the residential mission administrative offices.

b. Provide an occasion for the trainee to receive information concerning mission policy, housing suggestions, children's schooling, transportation concerns, and language school.

c. Allow related mission administrative staff an opportunity to brief the trainee concerning matters of sensitivity and other pertinent information related to residential work in the area.

5. Work time

Objective: To provide time for the trainee to complete work already started and/or to view the Global Evangelization Resource Video Tapes.

6. Evaluation interview

Objective: To give the trainee an understanding of how he or she is perceived by staff and peers, areas of strengths or weaknesses, and prospects for effective work.

Action Steps:

a. Provide evaluative information to the trainee from staff and peers.

b. Evaluate the trainee's attitude in training, progress in the development of Goals and Action Plans, and general preparedness to do nonresidential missionary work.

c. Provide affirmation and critical feedback to the trainee.

d. Devise goals for skill development and/or personal growth.

7. Work time

Objective: To provide the trainee with an opportunity to complete work still pending and/or view Global Evangelization Resource Video Tapes.

Training resources

Nonresidential missionary training programs are now being offered by several agencies. The Foreign Mission Board of the Southern Baptist Convention, Youth With A Mission (YWAM), and the Association of International Mission Services (AIMS) are each committed to the expansion and development of nonresidential missions to closed countries, and offer training to qualified applicants.

Though the nonresidential missionary movement is still in its infancy, it is growing rapidly. In hopes of further expanding the number of Christian missionaries involved in this diverse approach, YWAM and the AIMS have opened their doors to welcome all like-minded evangelicals to be a part of their training.

The Foreign Mission Board of the Southern Baptist Convention has agreed to help other Christian agencies to set up their own nonresidential missionary program by inviting a missionary trainer from any such agency to attend their four-and-a-half-week training program in Rockville, Virginia. Visiting trainers are encouraged to participate in every aspect of a nonresidential missionary training session, and then share in the growing network of nonresidential missionaries deployed throughout the world. Consequently, the number of agencies and individuals committed to this approach has grown steadily over the past three years, with even more agencies awaiting training in the upcoming sessions.

For more information, contact Youth With A Mission, P.O. Box 55309, Seattle, WA 98155 USA, (206) 283-1071, or P.O. Box YWAM, Kailua-Kona, Hawaii, 96745 USA, (808) 329-1621; contact the Association of International Mission Services (AIMS), P.O. Box 64534, Virginia Beach, VA 23464 USA, (804) 523-7979; contact the Foreign Mission Board of the Southern Baptist Convention, P.O. Box 6767, Richmond, VA 23230 USA, (804) 353-0151.

Passing the torch

It is impossible to do justice to the whole concept of nonresidential missionary training in a brief prospectus. The joys of discovery which occur each step of the way; the late nights tinkering with newly discovered desktop publishing techniques; the incessant brainstorming sessions about strategies and resources; the serious discussions over matters of security and confidentiality; the deepening bond between the nonresidential missionary trainee and the population target and between one nonresidential missionary and another—all of this escapes description in a syllabus, yet is at the heart of the ministry.

A common experience of nonresidential missionary trainees as they enter into the world of their population target—and the history of efforts to reach that target—is a growing awareness of the legacy that has preceded them, and to which they are now adding their contribution.

One nonresidential missionary trainee began his networking with other Christian agencies by sending out over 200 letters to mission agencies working in Asia. The trainee knew that his people group had never received the benefit of a Scripture translation; both Wycliffe and the United Bible Societies recorded no Scripture portions at all.

After an appropriate time, the trainee began receiving responses from the various agencies to whom he had written. Each one that responded confessed they had no work among his target population nor did they know of anyone else working with the group. Almost all of them, however, went on to say that they would pray for the trainee and speak to other agencies and individuals which might provide further information. Within a few weeks, a second wave of letters began arriving to the trainee. These were the fruits of his networking, yet came from individuals he had never met nor written. Most of them were simple words of encouragement and promises to pray for his efforts.

One letter was different. It came from England from an elderly retired missionary named William Scott. The letter was hand-written in an old man's shaky scrawl. "Dear brother," it began, "I was a missionary to the people you are now trying to reach. Before the Communist revolution 40 years ago, I was sent by my mission board to evangelize this people. I am now 82 years old." As the trainee read the letter, he felt his heart beat more rapidly. Then he read the words, "I have been praying for these people all these years—that God would raise up new laborers for the harvest. You see, when I was younger, I led some of them to Christ and planted churches among them. I never knew if anyone would ever be able to follow up on my work."

The letter continued, "Before I was expelled from the country, I translated the Gospel of Mark into their language. I know that God had a purpose in my preserving this little translation all these years. When I left the country I was body-searched nine times, but miraculously the book was never discovered! I'm sad to say that for the past 40 years no one would take my translation and publish it. I spoke to Bible Societies and mission agencies and no one saw any possibilities of completing the translation. And so, for forty years it has sat in my desk drawer. But now I am sending it to you. God bless you, my brother."

The legacy of transmitting the faith from one generation to another continued for that same trainee two years later. After successfully placing some Christian tentmakers among his population target, he heard from them the story of a young man who was struggling with accepting the Christian faith.

One of the tentmakers told the trainee the story. "Liu was always asking us questions about the Bible, Jesus, prayer and the Christian faith," he said. "He was like a sponge wanting to know more and more and yet he couldn't make a commitment to believe. The Christians didn't push Liu to make a decision. Instead, they urged him to pray and ask God to reveal himself. When the time came for the annual spring holiday, Liu decided to return to his village for a week and ask his parents for their advice. Liu's parents had grown up under the atheistic ideology of Communism, and strongly advised Liu to forget the superstitious Christian faith—it could only bring him trouble.

"Later that week, Liu accompanied his parents to their ancestral cemetery. The school holiday, commemorated throughout much of Asia, was a time for sweeping the graves of the ancestors. It was there that God chose to reveal himself. As Liu pulled the weeds away from the tombstone of his grandfather, he was stunned to see the image of a cross and a Christian benediction engraved on the marker. His grandfather had been a believer."

The nonresidential missionary blinked back the tears as he heard the story. In his mind's eye he saw another face—the face of old William Scott. He wondered if it had been that old missionary who had presented the gospel message to the now deceased grandfather.

The tentmaker concluded, "Now Liu has decided firmly that he will be baptized too."

## EIGHT

Does it really work?

WITH THE PROPER TRAINING and orientation, nonresidential missions offers a world of new possibilities where previously none existed. By this time, you should have an understanding of the definition of a nonresidential missionary, the nature of the work, the biblical and historical basis of the concept, its target focus and the kind of training that the nonresidential missionary must undergo. You have seen some descriptive illustrations of how the nonresidential missionary approach may be applied to different settings around the world. Some will still ask the question: "But does it really work?"

Though situations and individuals vary and the history of nonresidential missions is still in its infancy, the answer to this question still comes back a resounding, "Yes!" In situation after situation, newly deployed nonresidential missionaries have set out to reach the world's most inhospitable assignments: Afghanistan, Saudi Arabia, the Soviet Union, China, Iran. The stories they have brought back, even in this brief time, fill us with hope and enthusiasm over what God has chosen to do with this new approach to the age-old challenge of world evangelization.

As new nonresidential missionaries are deployed to an increasing number of the worlds' more than 3000 unevangelized peoples and cities, we look forward to even more delightful reports of God's blessings echoing back from the ends of the earth.

As a final illustration, the reader is invited to examine two actual "before and after" case studies of nonresidential missions. Cause and effect in a field as large and complex as mission and evangelization can be difficult to establish. In order to address that very issue, however, two nonresidential missions cases were selected on the basis of the extremity of their isolation from Christian witness prior to the assignment. This makes it easier to track the effectiveness of the nonresidential missionary's contributions.

Once again it will be necessary to shield the exact identities of those persons involved and the place of their ministry. Unlike the previous illustrations, however, which used a composite of nonresidential ministries from various settings around the world, the following two stories actually happened in their respective situations.

Before and after among the Altai

As their name suggests, the Altai are related to the vast Turko-Mongolian Altaic family of peoples stretching from the Korean peninsula in the east, across Manchuria, Mongolia and Soviet Central Asia, until reaching its western-most extremes in the Anatolian peninsula of modern day Turkey. The Altai are a predominantly Muslim people residing in a socialist country far from a sizeable Christian witness of any type.

Even before they adopted a restrictive socialist form of government, the Altai had never had much exposure to Christianity. A major reason for this isolation has been their geographical insulation. Literally tens of millions of non-Christian Muslim or Buddhist peoples form thick barriers around them, preventing missionaries from reaching them with the gospel for centuries.

In 1988, a nonresidential missionary was assigned to the Altai and began studying their condition. He soon discovered that they had no Scripture in their own language, no indigenous churches in their own language, and no Christian missionaries of any denomination attempting to reach them. Within two months, the nonresidential missionary had determined the most strategic location from which to base his family and begin his work.

Tapping into his denominational prayer resources, the nonresidential missionary made sure that supporting churches in the United States had "Altai People Profiles" and were committed to praying for the Altai people. Within six months, 300 churches had committed to regular prayer for the Altai people.

During his first month on the job, he visited the capital city of the Altai province, and initiated an educational exchange program with the regional Ministry of Education. This program would allow anywhere from 25-50 students, educators and researchers from an association of evangelical universities in the West to enter Altai universities.

Two months later, the nonresidential missionary placed his first exchange students—a Danish family engaged in translating the Bible into Altai language. Because it was understood to be a scholarly linguistic undertaking, the translation projection received the full blessing of the Altai ministry of education.

Six months later, the nonresidential missionary organized and led a delegation of Christian business persons from three Western countries who want to establish ministry presence within the country. One of the business representatives is developing the contacts necessary to produce a translation and dubbing of a film about Jesus, with hopes that marketing and distribution will be able to proceed through legitimate film distribution channels in the Altai province.

Another business representative opened an international trade office between the Altai province and other countries. Special trade concessions allow the trade office to employ numerous Christian traders, each engaged in evangelism and church planting along with their legitimate business pursuits. Plans are already being implemented for graduate business students to study and learn the Altai language through the auspices of the exchange program, and then to transfer into the trade office for purposes of ongoing evangelism and church planting opportunities.

A recent natural disaster in the Altai province has left thousands of Altai people homeless, facing many months of malnutrition and possible starvation. Requesting human needs funding from Western Christian agencies, the nonresidential missionary has been able to initiate agriculture development projects that will begin to meet the needs of the people and promise opportunities for face-to-face ministry and witness for many years to come.

Because the nonresidential missionary has established numerous ways of retaining a residence in the Altai province, and is coordinating all of them through a centrally-monitored strategy, he is able to ensure that if somebody loses a residence permit under one program, he will be able to transfer into another.

To strengthen prayer support for the Altai, and continue to provide the necessary personnel to fill the many openings that have emerged, the nonresidential missionary has developed a "partnership program" with an association of sixty churches in the United States.

At the time of this writing, presence has been secured for a number of witnesses to the Altai people. On Christmas Day 1990—just two years after the beginning of a nonresidential ministry to the Altai—40 to 50 Christian tentmakers, students and friendship evangelists from a dozen countries and Christian traditions celebrated the Lord's birthday in the capital city of the Altai province. They have been allowed to live and work there as a result of one nonresidential missionary's efforts. They share the hope of being joined soon by the first fruits of God's harvest among the Altai people.

Before and after among the Xiao

In 1987, an overseas mission board from the United States deployed its first nonresidential missionary to the Xiao people. His research revealed them to be one of the least evangelized peoples on earth. They are sixteen million strong and living in a remote province of Asia.

The Xiao live under a highly restrictive Communist government that has allowed no missionaries for most of this century. The Xiao comprise one of the largest peoples in Asia and the largest language community in the world with no Christian Scripture whatsoever in their own language.

Upon further investigation, the nonresidential missionary discovered that of the more than 80 mission agencies with work of some kind in or around the country where the Xiao live, none directly work with the Xiao. The Xiao have no missionaries, no Bible, no Christian institutions such as hospitals, clinics or schools, no gospel radio broadcasts, and no known organized efforts of intercession on their behalf. In short, at the time that a nonresidential missionary was assigned to them, the Xiao stood very near to zero on the evangelization scale.

Within a year, using the prayer program of his denomination, the nonresidential missionary had more than 500 churches committed to faithful prayer for the Xiao.

In 1989, the Xiao were featured in a worldwide denominational day of prayer and fasting for world evangelization, and were the subject of the prayers of tens of thousands of faithful Christians around the world.

Stimulated by a brochure on the Xiao developed by the nonresidential missionary, the Xiao have also been adopted for prayer by other Christian groups such as Youth With A Mission and the Lausanne II Congress on World Evangelization at Manila.

Recognizing the Xiao province as one of the poorest regions in Asia, a statewide Christian men's organization based in the United States has made an agreement with the provincial government where the Xiao live to build a hospital in the province. One of the fundamental assurances from the government has been that this hospital could have a Christian identity and Christian witness.

Two medical nurses serving in a Christian mission of a neighboring country have established a relationship with a nursing school in the capital city of the Xiao province, where they have been able to share both medical skills and a Christian witness.

When the nonresidential missionary made it known to other Christian agencies that the Xiao were the largest people in the world with no Scripture, a Scripture translation agency stepped forward with a commitment to begin a translation. This was followed by a major Bible publishing society pledging to publish the translation when it is completed. Several other agencies agreed to help deliver the Bible to the Xiao people.

Because there is only one school in the world which teaches the Xiao language, the nonresidential missionary traveled to the school, established a friendly relationship with the school's administration, and secured an invitation for two recruited students with doctoral degrees in linguistics to enroll in the school and begin a translation of the Bible into the Xiao language.

Realizing that many of the remote Xiao villages would never be open to Western Christian presence, the nonresidential missionary developed a cooperative interdenominational project team. This team united his own denominational agency, an interdenominational radio broadcasting company and a Christian literature distribution agency to begin gospel radio broadcasting in the Xiao language. Making this goal a reality has required building extensive networks, including Western funding and the use of Two-Thirds World Christians to record the testimonies of local Xiao believers, since there are no Xiao speakers living anywhere outside the country.

A further important step occurred when the nonresidential missionary was able to network with South Korean Christians who have agreed to manufacture and deliver "portable missionaries"—radio receivers that are pre-set to receive the broadcast when it is transmitted.

In 1990, the first Xiao radio broadcasts went on the air. They reach the Xiao people five times a week for thirty minutes, teaching about Jesus Christ in the language of the people. The broadcasts are timed to reach the people when they arrive home in the evenings from their day in the rice fields. These are the only radio broadcasts of any type in the language of the Xiao people.

As a result of the nonresidential missionary's initiative, the Xiao translation of film about Jesus has risen to the status of top priority for Asia. With the help of the film, many of the Xiao who are unable to read will be able to see and hear the life of Jesus portrayed in their own language before their very eyes.

Responding to a local request for English teachers, the nonresidential missionary has generated and implemented an English Language Institute project, allowing three teams of 20-30 Christians to spend their summer living among the Xiao, teaching English and sharing a witness face to face with the people.

Utilizing his mission board's intermediate term missions program, the nonresidential missionary has placed three seminary-trained young women, each with two years of overseas cross-cultural missionary experience, in teaching assignments among the Xiao, sharing their faith in an appropriate manner with a goal of seeing indigenous Christian communities emerge. Within three months, they have led the first Xiao to Christ.

By the end of the first year among the Xiao, the number of converts has risen to three. Each of the young missionary-educators report their amazement with how hungry the people are to hear the gospel message.

In addition to these individual converts to Christ, the nonresidential missionary's contributions in terms of prayer, Scripture translation and radio broadcasting have created a "climate of evangelization" in which the Xiao are learning about the Gospel of Jesus Christ through a range of media for the first time.

As a result of many factors—including the work of the nonresidential missionary, recent political upheavals in the country, and, most importantly, the providence of God—changes are coming to the Xiao people.

In 1989, roughly two years after the beginning of the nonresidential ministry to the Xiao, a knowledgeable local Christian leader working in the Xiao province reported that a great turning of the people is underway. Already across the province, 3,000 people have been baptized into the church this year, and scores more await baptism. This is more than four times the total number of baptisms from the previous year.

By mid-1990, the Christian leader reported that God is doing a remarkable work among the Xiao. They have become the fastest growing sector of the church in this multi-ethnic province. Numbers of Christian Xiao have swollen from fewer than 13,000 to more than 30,000 over the past few years.

This local Christian leader knows nothing of the nonresidential missionary effort to reach his people. He is simply grateful that God has chosen to pour out his blessings upon them.

Prior to this nonresidential missionary's efforts, the Xiao were an unevangelized and largely unknown people to the outside Christian world. Today, they are the prayer focus of hundreds of churches and thousands of Christians around the world. And as a direct result of nonresidential missionary efforts, more than a dozen evangelical Christian agencies now have evangelistic ministries aimed at reaching the Xiao.

Transformed lives

The stories of the Altai and the Xiao peoples offer some of the first fruits of what will hopefully follow throughout the unevangelized world. Numbers of converts are not the ultimate goal of the program, but rather the individual souls and lives that those numbers represent.

Last year, one of the Christian workers living among the Xiao had the privilege of leading a young Xiao woman to Christ. The story of this young Xiao believer is indicative of the entire effort.

As she invited Christ into her life, the young Xiao woman said, "All my life people have told me that there was no God. I knew that there must be a God, but I never had a guide to show me how to know him."

As a result of one nonresidential missionary's persistent efforts, this young woman now knows the living God. On Christmas Day, she was baptized into a local Christian church. She has already begun sharing her faith with her relatives in a remote Xiao village.

Due to the flexibility and scope of the nonresidential method, new developments in the program are unfolding every few weeks. Because nonresidential missionary practitioners wish to remain innovative and pragmatic, they have adopted a descriptive rather than prescriptive posture as they apply this concept to diverse settings throughout the world and continually monitor the effort. With each passing month, it becomes more and more difficult to compile a survey of what even one nonresidential missionary has accomplished, much less a comprehensive overview of the work around the world.

One thing is clear: the nonresidential missionary approach is making a difference. A world of peoples who would otherwise continue to wait for the chance to hear and respond to Jesus are beginning to receive it through the assistance of nonresidential missionaries. Millions more have yet to have their chance.

Since the concept was first launched in 1986, the number of nonresidential missionaries has increased steadily until nearly one hundred nonresidential missionaries live and/or work in thirty countries—from the Muslims of North Africa to the Indonesian archipelago—projecting a Christian witness to nearly 200 million of the world's least evangelized cities and peoples.

Despite the growing number of agencies and individuals committed to nonresidential missions, it is still true that only about one percent of the world's unevangelized peoples are currently engaged by nonresidential missionaries. Part Two of this book is provided to help locate the rest of the people in the world without access to the gospel. Chapter nine lists the world's least evangelized countries, cities, and peoples. Chapter ten breaks down the overwhelming figure of 1.3 billion people into twelve related complexes with a corresponding array of related Christian resources.

PART TWO

THE PEOPLE TO BE SERVED

NINE

People waiting for good news

TWO OF THE MOST COMMONLY ASKED QUESTIONS regarding the people in the world without access to the gospel are, "Where are they?" and "Who are they?" Before these questions can be answered we must begin with a clear understanding of what it means to be *evangelized* and *unevangelized*. These words are used today to refer to everything from "exposed to the gospel" to "actively involved in a church."

In a most basic sense—the meaning that will be adhered to here—people who are *evangelized* have had the gospel or *evangelion* presented to them. Thus, the antonym, *unevangelized*, encompasses those who have not had the gospel presented to them. Given the myriad means by which the gospel can now be communicated—through radio, television, missions, local churches, Christian literature, the Bible, video cassettes, audio cassettes, etc.—to say that a people are unevangelized is to place them in a virtual desert of gospel witness. Despite nearly two thousand years of missionary activity since the first pronouncement of the Great Commission, such places do still exist.

Without good news in countries

We have already seen that the unevangelized world consists of 1.3 billion individuals who have never heard the gospel of Jesus Christ. While these people live throughout the world, they are by no means equally distributed. The great majority of the world's unevangelized peoples live in fifty of the world's least evangelized countries. It is no coincidence that the same countries are among the least amenable to missionary presence. On the following page is a table listing of the world's 30 least evangelized countries, where over half of the population has no access to the gospel of Jesus Christ.[1]

---

1   Information listed in this table is derived from David Barrett and Todd Johnson's *Our Globe and How to Reach It* (Birmingham, Alabama: New Hope, 1990).

THIRTY LEAST EVANGELIZED COUNTRIES

Column 1 gives the current United Nations name for the country in alphabetical order, *Column 2* shows the country's 1990 population, *Column 3* is an estimated percent of the country's population who are unevangelized, and *Column 4* is an estimate of the number of unevangelized persons in the country.

Country	1990 Pop	% Unevang	Unevang Pop
Afghanistan	16,557,000	83	13,742,000
Albania	3,245,000	63	2,044,000
Algeria	25,364,000	71	18,008,000
Bahrain	515,000	54	278,000
Bangladesh	115,593,000	54	62,420,000
Bhutan	1,516,000	83	1,258,000
Cambodia	8,246,000	74	6,102,000
China	1,135,496,000	51	579,103,000
Comoros	457,000	60	274,000
Guinea	6,876,000	80	5,501,000
Iran	56,585,000	68	38,478,000
Iraq	18,920,000	65	12,298,000
Laos	4,071,000	60	2,446,000
Libya	4,544,000	82	3,726,000
Maldives	215,000	81	174,000
Mauritania	2,024,000	89	1,801,000
Mongolia	2,227,000	85	1,893,000
Morocco	24,922,000	67	17,698,000
Nepal	19,143,000	62	11,869,000
Niger	7,109,000	79	5,616,000
North Korea	22,937,000	72	16,515,000
North Yemen	8,017,000	82	6,574,000
Oman	1,468,000	81	1,189,000
Pakistan	122,666,000	52	63,579,000
Sahara	178,000	87	155,000
Saudi Arabia	14,131,000	66	9,327,000
Somalia	7,555,000	82	6,195,000
South Yemen	2,491,000	72	1,794,000
Tunisia	8,169,000	69	5,637,000
Turkey	55,616,000	71	39,487,000

Without good news in cities

Within these highly restricted and largely unevangelized countries, a further demographic development is taking place—they are becoming urbanized. Throughout the world, the history of the twentieth century has been one of urbanization. In part a product of enormous population growth, urbanization is also a reflection of the increasing interdependence of global economies. This fact should not be lost on the discerning missionary. Today, all of the world's great cities are inextricably linked to one another through trade, communications and the simple fact that they share a common environment.

Free-market cities in the Western world are often matched with urban counterparts in the Socialist world through "sister-city" programs. These informal relationships between cities serve to enhance the flow of persons and ideas between otherwise disparate peoples. Tashkent (Uzbek, S.S.R.) and Seattle, Washington; Baku (Azerbaijan, S.S.R.) and Houston, Texas; Alma Ata (Kazakh, S.S.R.) and Tucson, Arizona are but a few of the many, many "sister-city" relationships that have developed over the years between cities of the East and West. Their initial purpose was to stimulate trade and understanding, but with this open door have also come numerous opportunities for Christian witness and ministry.

Over the past few years, missiologists have increasingly awakened to the strategic importance of the urban world. As new missionaries are sent into the world, they are typically deployed to capitals and other major urban centers. The gospel is able to emanate from these centers to surrounding provinces and regions. There is no reason why this valid strategy should be limited to traditional residential missions in open countries. The same principle applies to unevangelized, closed countries as well. Accordingly, an increasing number of nonresidential missionaries adopt assignments to unevangelized cities and seek to serve a people through them.

Tragically for the cause of world evangelization, most of these great metropolises remain totally unknown to the Christian world. Ironically, once revealed and targeted by nonresidential missionaries, they tend to be easier to reach than many of the world's remote and sprawling unevangelized peoples. The following table lists the world's fifty least evangelized *megacities* (cities of over a million population).[2] Again, by "evangelized," we mean they have been confronted with the gospel of Jesus Christ and have had an opportunity to respond to it.

---

2   Information listed in this table is derived from the *World Evangelization Database* of the Southern Baptist Convention's Foreign Mission Board.

FIFTY LEAST EVANGELIZED CITIES WITH OVER 800,000 PEOPLE

Column 1 ranks the cities, with the least evangelized listed first. Column 2 gives the city's name, with variants listed in parenthesis. Column 3 lists the country in which the city is located. Column 4 gives the estimated current population size of the city. Column 5 projects the population of the city for the year 2000. Column 6 gives an estimate of the number of people in the city affiliated with some type of Christian church (rounded to the nearest thousand). Column 7 provides the Anglicized name for the predominant language of the city. Column 8 gives an estimate of the number of unevangelized people in the city (rounded to the nearest thousand).

#	City	Country	Pop 1990	Pop 2000	Ch Affil	Language	Unevang
1	Konya (Iconium)	Turkey	823,887	985,276	20	Turkish	614,000
2	Adana (Ataniya, Seyhan)	Turkey	1,030,058	1,231,834	900	Turkish	676,000
3	Mashhad (Meshed)	Iran	1,078,290	1,370,739	1,500	Farsi	664,000
4	Tianjin (Tientsin)	China	8,283,193	9,256,701	78,000	Putonghua	5,843,000
5	Urumqi (Wulumuchi, Luntai)	China	1,047,283	1,170,369	4,000	Uygur/Putonghua	699,000
6	Anshan	China	1,302,614	1,455,708	12,000	Putonghua	862,000
7	Benxi (Penki, Pen-hsi)	China	842,974	942,047	8,000	Putonghua	558,000
8	Dalian (Luda, Dairen)	China	1,612,787	1,802,335	15,000	Putonghua	1,067,000
9	Guiyang (Kweiyang)	China	1,471,074	1,643,967	14,000	Putonghua	973,000
10	Tangshan	China	1,533,895	1,714,171	14,000	Putonghua	1,015,000
11	Changchun (Kuachengzi)	China	1,903,855	2,127,612	36,000	Korean	1,243,000
12	Changsha (Tan, Tanzhou)	China	1,161,463	1,297,968	11,000	Xiang	758,000
13	Fushun	China	1,291,039	1,442,772	12,000	Putonghua	843,000
14	Qiqihaer (Tsitsihar)	China	1,317,449	1,472,286	12,000	Putonghua	860,000
15	Shijiazhuang (Shihkia-chwong)	China	1,164,385	1,301,233	11,000	Putonghua	760,000
16	Daqing	China	826,341	923,460	8,000	Putonghua	539,000
17	Jixi (Chihsi)	China	851,852	951,969	9,000	Putonghua	554,000
18	Zhengzhou (Chengchow, Kiangan)	China	1,529,737	1,709,524	22,000	Putonghua	992,000
19	Chengdu (Chengtu, Yizhou)	China	2,919,222	3,262,313	55,000	Putonghua	1,753,000
20	Chongqing (Chungking)	China	2,818,192	3,149,408	53,000	Putonghua	1,875,000
21	Harbin (Haerbin, Huining)	China	2,781,106	3,107,964	52,000	Putonghua	1,767,000

#	City	Country	Pop 1990	Pop 2000	Ch Affil	Language	Unevang
22	Kunming (Yunnanfu)	China	1,545,695	1,727,358	29,000	Putonghua	995,000
23	Yichun (I-chun, Ichun)	China	823,532	920,320	16,000	Putonghua	530,000
24	Zaozhuang (Tsao-chuang)	China	1,355,434	1,514,735	26,000	Putonghua	873,000
25	Zibo (Tzupo, Tzepo, Zhangdian)	China	2,657,486	2,969,815	75,000	Putonghua	1,541,000
26	Zigong (Tzekung, Tzekun)	China	943,555	1,054,450	18,000	Putonghua	607,000
27	Hefei (Hofei, Lu, Luzhou)	China	866,686	968,546	16,000	Putonghua	550,000
28	Huainan (Hwainan)	China	1,121,343	1,253,132	21,000	Putonghua	712,000
29	Huhhot (Guisui, Kewisue)	China	821,621	918,185	23,000	Mongolian	522,000
30	Lupanshui (Liupanshui)	China	2,329,557	2,603,345	66,000	Putonghua	1,457,000
31	Nanchang (Hongzhou)	China	1,172,027	1,309,773	33,000	Gan	744,000
32	Nanning	China	969,515	1,083,461	18,000	Putonghua	615,000
33	Baotou (Paotaw, Paotow)	China	1,172,252	1,310,024	44,000	Mongolian	734,000
34	Jilin(Kirin, Chilin)	China	1,185,850	1,325,221	45,000	Korean	742,000
35	Pingxiang	China	1,295,534	1,447,796	24,000	Gan	811,000
36	Kabul	Afghan.	1,538,019	1,903,813	2,000	Pushtu	740,000
37	Haiphong	Vietnam	2,295,390	2,771,338	102,000	Vietnamese	1,296,000
38	Datong (Tatung)	China	1,048,632	1,171,876	39,000	Putonghua	647,000
39	Qingdao (Tsingtao)	China	1,277,328	1,427,450	48,000	Putonghua	788,000
40	Shenyang (Mukden, Fengtian)	China	4,339,388	4,849,388	82,000	Korean	2,651,000
41	Luoyang (Xijing, Honan)	China	1,036,832	1,158,689	39,000	Putonghua	630,000
42	Jaipur	India	1,175,879	1,370,524	4,000	Hindi	665,000
43	Tabriz	Iran	1,038,006	1,319,529	13,000	Azerbaijani	527,000
44	Xian (Hsian, Jingchao)	China	2,406,988	2,689,876	113,000	Putonghua	1,426,000
45	Taiyuan	China	1,902,170	2,125,728	108,000	Putonghua	1,122,000
46	Kanpur (Cawnpore)	India	2,181,696	2,542,836	15,000	Hindi	1,078,000
47	Multan	Pakistan	890,615	1,118,655	7,000	Urdu	456,000
48	Jinan (Ji, Qi, Licheng)	China	1,480,851	1,654,893	56,000	Putonghua	847,000
49	Surat	India	1,068,101	1,244,906	3,000	Urdu/Hindi	568,000
50	Nanjing (Nanking, Jinling)	China	2,257,857	2,523,219	106,000	Wu	1,283,000

A world of peoples

Despite a growing awareness of the need in cities, most Christian missioners continue to view the world in terms of countries or nations. Virtually every mission agency counts the number of countries it has entered and then congratulates or criticizes itself on that basis. Never mind that the agency might have a single missionary family living in a nation the size of Indonesia with 180 million inhabitants and another family living in New Caledonia with only 165,000 inhabitants. The bottom line is that both countries are "covered." Viewing the world in terms of political nations invariably leads to an unclear understanding of the world's complex nature.

From the vantage point of history, the emergence of political nations is a fairly recent phenomenon, accompanying the break-up of the Holy Roman Empire at the end of the Middle Ages. As these young European nations grew powerful and spread their influence around the world, they imposed political models similar to their own on the peoples they conquered. Often, these artificial political boundaries imposed from the West completely disregarded ancient demographic ties of race, language, culture and religion.

Since the collapse of Western colonial powers at the end of World War II, these contrived nations have begun to unravel like cheap woven cloth. Today, rather than diminishing, the pace of ethnic liberation movements has proceeded steadily.

Ethnic peoples such as Basques, Biafrans, Kanaks, Sikhs, Tadzhiks, Karens, Tamils, Cossacks, Mosquitos and Kurds persistently invade our consciousness even as they fill our newspapers with protests and revolts demanding that the world accept the fact that they are not Spaniards, Nigerians, New Caledonians, Indians, Russians, Burmese, Sri Lankans, Soviets, Nicaraguans, or Iranians. Instead, they have their own identity as a unique people, an ethnolinguistic family, deserving recognition for their own distinct culture and right to existence.

What does this mean for Christian missions? It may mean that we need to further adjust the lenses through which we view the world.

Clinging to artificial political models of the world can lead one to conclude that the Soviet Union is either Christian or not Christian. In fact, parts of the Soviet empire are celebrating over 1000 years of Christianity, while other areas have yet to hear the gospel for the first time. It is particularly those populous and geographically expansive nations such as the USSR, China, India, Indonesia and Nigeria that defy characterization as either Christian or non-Christian, evangelized or unevangelized. To understand them, we must get beyond their political facade of unity to see the diverse human mosaic within.

Rather than settling for these colonial models of national boundaries, we must begin to see the peoples of the world as they see themselves—as distinct ethnic and linguistic communities. Each people, no matter how remote, isolated or intractable, deserves its own Scripture, its own Christian witness and its own gospel-centered church translated into its own distinctive culture. This is serving the real world.

With the assistance of modern computer technology, it has become a relatively easy matter to catalog the world's great ethnolinguistic families in every country on earth. The table on the following pages lists the hundred least evangelized peoples with a population greater than 800,000.[3] Thanks again to the wealth of global information and the use of computer databases, we can know a great deal about these unevangelized population segments. We know who they are; we know where they live; we know what they are like. The remaining question is, how can we minister to them in the name of Jesus Christ?

---

3   Information in this table is derived from the *World Evangelization Database* of the Southern Baptist Foreign Mission Board.

HUNDRED LEAST EVANGELIZED PEOPLES WITH A POPULATION GREATER THAN 800,000

Column 1 ranks the world's least evangelized peoples of over 800,000 population. Column 2 gives the name of the ethnolinguistic people. Column 3 lists the country where the people live. Column 4 gives an estimate of the population of the people in 1990. Column 5 projects the number of people in the group by the year 2000, given current demographic trends. Column 6 gives the estimated number of individuals affiliated with a church or Christian community (including children of Christians), rounded to the nearest thousand (unless under 10,000 population). Column 7 lists the autoglossonymn, or name of the mother tongue of the people, specifically denoting what the people call their own language. Variant names are given in parenthesis. Column 8 is an estimate of the number of unevangelized individuals, rounded to the nearest thousand.

#	People	Country	Pop 1990	Pop 2000	Ch affil	Language	Unevang
1	Qashqai	Iran	848,776	1,116,907	20	Qashqai	798,000
2	Komering (Ogan)	Indonesia	1,083,083	1,249,973	20	Komering (Ogan)	996,000
3	Turkmen (Turkomani)	Iran	905,361	1,191,368	20	Turkmen (Anauli)	833,000
4	Beja (Beni-Amer, Ababda)	Sudan	1,160,102	1,547,531	0	Bedawye (Beja, Bedawiye)	1,066,000
5	Lamponger (Lampungese)	Indonesia	1,173,340	1,354,138	20	Lampung (Lampungese)	1,068,000
6	Bakhtiari	Iran	1,075,116	1,414,749	20	Bakhtiari (Luri)	978,000
7	Baluchi	Iran	1,244,872	1,638,130	10	Baluchi	1,108,000
8	Turkmen	Soviet Union	2,228,471	2,381,269	10	Turkmen (Jagarta)	1,961,000
9	Tadzhik	Afghanistan	3,923,912	6,306,087	10	Tadzhik (Galcha, Dari)	3,414,000
10	Chechen (Shishan, Kokhchi)	Soviet Union	830,565	887,514	10	Chechen	3,723,000
11	Achehnese (Aceh, Atjeh)	Indonesia	3,021,801	3,487,425	300	Aceh (Banda, Daja, Pase)	2,629,000
12	Khalka Mongol (Mongolian)	China	3,842,518	4,351,466	800	Khalka (Dariganga, Urat)	3,342,000
13	Northern Meo (Huayuan)	China	1,001,394	1,134,030	900	Hsianghsi Meo (Chiwei)	870,000
14	Tung (Dong, Kam)	China	1,605,023	1,817,611	1,600	Kam (Tung-chia, Tong)	1,395,000
15	Gilaki	Iran	3,281,934	4,318,707	10	Gilaki (Gelaki, Gilani)	2,822,000
16	Kortha Bihari	India	1,706,746	2,085,059	200	Kortha Magahi	1,468,000
17	Manchu	China	4,842,095	5,483,438	1,000	Sibo (Manchu, Juchen)	4,163,000
18	Nagpuri Bihari (Sadri)	India	1,898,755	2,319,628	400	Sadan (Nagpuri, Dikkukaji)	1,633,000

#	People	Country	Pop 1990	Pop 2000	Ch affil	Language	Unevang
19	Central Kurd	Iran	1,131,702	1,489,209	300	Mukri (Eastern, Kermanji)	973,000
20	Southern Kurd (Carduchi)	Iran	2,829,254	3,723,024	1,400	Kerman-shahi (Kurdi)	2,432,000
21	Chinese Tai	China	995,943	1,127,858	1,000	Chinese Tai	856,000
22	Zhuang (Chuang, Chwang)	China	15,067,689	17,063,429	15,000	Chwang (Chuang, Yungpei)	12,943,000
23	Brahui	Pakistan	908,711	1,203,557	1,800	Brahui	780,000
24	Tujia (Tuchia)	China	3,190,516	3,613,105	13,000	Tuchia	2,731,000
25	Baluchi	Pakistan	3,671,227	4,862,416	20	Baluchi	3,121,000
26	Fula Jalon (Futa Dyalon)	Guinea	1,920,465	2,479,998	200	Futa Jalo (Pulaar)	1,632,000
27	North Central Gond	India	854,476	1,043,630	300	Chhindwara Gondi	725,000
28	Northern Gond (Betul)	India	852,270	1,041,440	250	Betul Gondu (Koitor, Gandi)	725,000
29	Central Gond (Ghond)	India	853,373	1,042,520	300	Mandla Gondi	725,000
30	I (Yi, Lolo)	China	6,142,124	6,955,658	6,000	Nesu (Lolo, I, Yi)	5,215,000
31	Nimadi (Nimari)	India	1,236,964	1,511,147	1,200	Nimadi (Nemadi, Bhuani)	1,050,000
32	Wagdi (Wagheri, Vagdi)	India	1,471,898	1,798,155	1,500	Wagdi (Vagi, Wagholi)	1,250,000
33	Kazakh	China	927,473	1,050,318	10	Hasaka (Kazakh)	779,000
34	Uzbek	Afghanistan	877,499	1,410,222	90	Uzbek (Kypchak)	737,000
35	Garhwali (Central Pahari)	India	853,373	1,042,530	260	Tehri	717,000
36	Hazara (Berberi)	Afghanistan	1,059,622	1,702,910	500	Hazaragi (Afghan Persian)	890,000
37	Bagri (Bahgri)	India	1,644,023	2,008,433	1,600	Bagri (Baorias)	1,379,000
38	Mina	India	2,243,517	2,740,810	6,700	Mina	1,878,000
39	Fula (Peuhala)	Mali	834,731	1,128,569	6,300	Massina (Fula, Peuhala)	695,000
40	Bazaar Low Malay Creole	Indonesia	1,263,597	1,458,302	130	Pasar Melayu (Bazaar, Low)	1,049,000
41	Northern Kurd (Kermanji)	Turkey	5,005,481	5,995,993	500	Zaza (Dimli, Gurmanji)	4,154,000
42	Kirghiz	Soviet Union	2,094,267	2,237,864	400	Kirghiz (Kara, Black)	1,738,000
43	Northern Kurd	Iraq	2,819,059	3,924,461	2,000	Kermanji (Hakari, Jezire)	2,338,000
44	Rajasthani (Mewari)	India	853,373	1,042,530	850	Mewari	707,000
45	Lamani (Banjara, Labhani)	India	1,874,092	2,289,499	2,400	Lamani (Lambadi, Kora)	1,553,000
46	Western Kurd (Kermanji)	Syria	958,115	1,349,743	1,200	Kermanji (Kurdi)	794,000

#	People	Country	Pop 1990	Pop 2000	Ch affil	Language	Unevang
47	Hani	China	1,192,498	1,350,446	48,000	Hani (Woni, Ho, Haw)	978,000
48	Makassarese (Macassar)	Indonesia	3,068,734	3,541,590	100	Macassar (Mengkasara)	2,516,000
49	Somali	Ethiopia	2,451,555	3,210,069	200	Somali (Soomaali)	2,010,000
50	Tadzhik	Soviet Union	3,184,311	3,402,649	300	Tadzhik	2,611,000
51	Garhwali (Pahari Gashwali)	India	1,135,669	1,387,398	200	Srinagaria (Gadwahi)	931,000
52	Afshari (Afsar)	Iran	848,776	1,116,907	300	Azeri (Azerbaijani)	696,000
53	Afghan Persian (Kaboli)	Iran	1,584,382	2,084,893	800	Dari (Kaboli, Khorasani)	1,298,000
54	Central Bhil	India	3,942,583	4,816,486	11,900	Bhili (Bhilori)	3,221,000
55	Ho	India	1,167,756	1,426,597	6,400	Ho (Lanka Kol, Lohara)	951,000
56	Bai (Pai, Minchia)	China	1,274,026	1,442,773	25,500	Pai (Minchia, Minkia)	1,032,000
57	Puyi (Bouyei, Pu-I)	China	2,388,288	2,704,621	23,900	Chungchia (Dioi, Jui, Igen)	1,935,000
58	Uighur (Kashgar)	China	6,709,418	7,598,091	20	Wei Wuer (I-kha, Lop)	5,435,000
59	Halebi Gypsy	Egypt	864,952	1,067,360	90	Masri (Mashriqi)	701,000
60	Zerma (Dyerma)	Niger	1,185,835	1,626,372	100	Zarma (Dyerma, Adzerma)	960,000
61	Kanuri	Nigeria	4,452,834	6,270,468	400	Kanuri	3,606,000
62	Han Chinese (Hainanese)	China	5,109,731	5,786,524	20,000	Wanning (Wenchang)	4,118,000
63	Lu (Pai-i)	China	881,145	997,854	18,000	Lu (Pai-i, Tai, Lu)	705,000
64	Bedouin	Egypt	1,081,190	1,334,200	20	Badawi (Bedouin Arabic)	865,000
65	Eastern Bhil (Vil)	India	2,371,609	2,897,294	2,400	Dehwali Bhili (Bhilbari)	1,895,000
66	Rajasthani (Bikaneri)	India	853,373	1,042,530	1,000	Bikaneri	682,000
67	Kumaoni (Central Pahari)	India	1,923,247	2,349,549	7,700	Kumauni (Kumgoni, Kummam)	1,531,000
68	Eastern Meo (Black, Heh)	China	2,048,207	2,319,496	10,000	Ch'ientung Miao	1,628,000
69	Western Meo (Peh, Hwa, Tak)	China	2,617,204	2,963,857	13,000	Ch'uan-ch'ientien Miao	2,081,000
70	Madurese	Indonesia	11,331,753	13,077,843	178,000	Bankalan (Madurese)	9,001,000
71	Banjarese	Indonesia	1,435,085	1,656,214	20	Banjar	1,134,000
72	Azerbaijani (Turk)	Iran	7,158,012	9,419,250	40	Azeri (Tabris, Moqaddan)	5,655,000
73	Sab	Somalia	815,936	1,058,755	20	Somali (Sab)	636,000
74	Hamyan Bedouin	Algeria	1,770,399	2,320,674	200	Badawi (Bedouin Arabic)	1,381,000

#	People	Country	Pop 1990	Pop 2000	Ch affil	Language	Unevang
75	Minangkabau	Indonesia	6,679,010	7,708,167	1,000	Minangkabau	5,208,000
76	Bororo (Western Fulani)	Nigeria	1,695,242	2,387,234	800	Fulfulde	1,321,000
77	Yao	China	1,579,815	1,789,064	11,000	Yao (Mien, Man, Taipan)	1,221,000
78	Pattani Malay	Thailand	934,951	1,068,700	200	Malay Pattani	720,000
79	Southern Bhil	India	1,116,382	1,363,837	4,000	Valvi Bhili	855,000
80	Okinawan	Japan	802,470	839,181	23,000	Luchu (Central, Ryukyuan)	611,000
81	Tulu (Tullu, Thulu, Tal)	India	1,801,812	2,201,197	18,000	Tulu (Tilu, Tuluva Bhasa)	1,369,000
82	Azerbaijani (Azurbijan)	Soviet Union	6,018,426	6,431,089	50	Azeri (Azerbaijani)	4,574,000
83	Tamang (Tamar, Sain)	Nepal	946,002	1,190,174	500	Tamang	718,000
84	Dogri (Hindi Dogri)	India	1,852,161	2,262,706	1,900	Dogri (Dhogaryali)	1,406,000
85	Kui (Khondi, Kond)	India	2,560,119	3,127,589	28,000	Kui (Khand, Kodu, Kodulu)	1,943,000
86	Tatar (Kazan Tatar)	Soviet Union	6,941,436	7,417,386	104,000	Kazan Tatar	5,241,000
87	Han Chinese (Hakka)	China	4,541,983	5,143,576	45,000	Sankiang (Sam Kiong)	3,406,000
88	Han Chinese (Hakka)	China	1,135,496	1,285,894	11,000	Tingchow	852,000
89	Kazakh	Soviet Union	7,204,083	7,698,042	700	Kazakh (Western, Kirghiz)	5,402,000
90	Hindustani	India	853,373	1,042,530	400	Hindustani	640,000
91	Sokoto Fulani	Nigeria	1,921,274	2,705,532	1,900	Fulfulde (Sokoto)	1,439,000
92	Hui (Dungan, Tunya)	China	8,131,059	9,208,031	10	Kuoyu (Mandarin)	6,017,000
93	Maninka (South Malinke)	Guinea	1,736,739	2,242,742	17,000	Maninka (Manding, Malinke)	1,285,000
94	Turkish Kurd	Turkey	4,449,317	5,329,772	400	Turkce (Turkish)	3,292,000
95	Iranian Kurd	Iran	3,395,105	4,467,628	1,000	Farsi (Persian)	2,511,000
96	Zott Gypsy (Nawar)	Iran	1,075,116	1,414,749	10	Arabiya (Arabic)	785,000
97	Ceylon Moor	Sri Lanka	1,122,913	1,264,839	10	Tamil	820,000
98	Crimean Tatar	Turkey	3,893,152	4,663,550	390	Turkce (Turkish)	2,842,000
99	Khalka Mongol	Mongolia	1,484,078	1,996,613	400	Khalka (Mongolian)	1,083,000
100	Arabized Berber	Egypt	1,081,190	1,334,200	1,000	Masri (Mashriqi)	788,000

Pieces of the task

Whether viewed in terms of countries, cities or peoples, each of these population segments represents a concrete ministry assignment that a nonresidential missionary may take on. As the missionary focuses on and serves one of these segments, he or she is able to set goals for progress that can be monitored. The next chapter shows how these individual ministry assignments can be woven together into a strategy spanning the unevangelized world.

## TEN

Wanted: twelve alliances for ministry

VIRTUALLY ALL OF THE GREAT UNEVANGELIZED PEOPLES of the world live in the eastern hemisphere in a massive belt, stretching from the Saharan Sahel of West Africa through the Middle East and Central Asia, and then eastward to encompass most of China to the north and India, Indochina and Indonesia to the south (see map on page 87). The inhabitants of this great belt include Muslims, Chinese traditional religionists, Indochinese Buddhists and South AsianHindus and tribal religionists.

When viewed as a whole, the challenge of 1.3 billion unevangelized people is staggering. Even when seen in their component parts of 3,030 distinct unevangelized cities, countries and peoples, the task appears daunting. An early concern of nonresidential mission administrators and strategists was the potential loneliness of a nonresidential missionary assignment. As the work unfolded, however, it was interesting to observe the natural alliances and relationships that evolved on the field.

These alliances reflected the existence of twelve related complexes of unevangelized peoples, and a corresponding array of Christian resources related to them. While nonresidential missionaries serving completely separate Berber peoples in North Africa might work independently of one another, they invariably found themselves locating the same key centers for Berber evangelization and the same strategic bases for establishing their place of residence. The same proved true for those serving Muslims in South Asia, peoples and cities in South China, the Arabic-speaking world, etc.

By carefully analyzing and cataloging these evolving patterns of nonresidential ministry, we can identify twelve distinct unevangelized population complexes stretching across the world from west Africa to northeast China.

The significance of this discovery for developing a global strategy of nonresidential mission has been considerable. Instead of sending out individual nonresidential missionaries into a yawning vortex of 3,030 countries, they are now deployed as members of one of twelve distinct teams.

A nonresidential missionary seeking to serve the Fula Jalon of Guinea, for example, becomes part of a "West African Team" of nonresidential missionaries, some of whom will be serving the Hausa or Kanuri of Nigeria; others the city of Tomboctou or the White Moors of Mauritania. Likewise, a newly deployed nonresidential missionary to the Yi people of Yunnan Province in China will join a "South China Team" consisting of nonresidential missionaries to the cities of Changsha or Nanning, or to the Meo or Puyi peoples also in the same region.

The following page provides an overview map of the unevangelized world broken down into twelve population complexes. The rest of the chapter provides maps and detailed information about each of the twelve complexes.

TWELVE UNEVANGELIZED POPULATION COMPLEXES

Each of the complexes identified in the map on page 87 shares affinities of geography, ethnicity, linguistics, historical-political ties or religious ties. Consequently, nonresidential missionaries seeking to serve any one of the cities or peoples within a given complex will find the need to gain access to related resources for ministry, evangelism, communication and travel. Complexes include:

1) West African Muslim Peoples
2) North African Berber Peoples
3) Arabic Peoples
4) East African Cushitic Peoples
5) Kurdo-Iranian Peoples
6) Turkic Peoples
7) South Asian Muslim Peoples
8) South Asian Hindustani Peoples
9) Southern China Peoples
10) Northern China Peoples
11) Indochina Peoples
12) Indo-Malaysian Peoples

The following pages include maps to help locate these complexes, along with more detailed information, and a closer look at one of the peoples within each complex. Numbers on the maps represent the places where the concentration of persons within the people group is highest. All figures for 1990 population, church membership, and unevangelized population are approximations based on the best research available.

WEST AFRICAN MUSLIM PEOPLES

The West African Muslim population complex is found in a dozen West African nations, stretching from the borders of Cameroon in the south to the desert reaches of Mauritania in the north. Nonresidential missionaries seeking to serve any of the peoples in this cluster will find an Islamic assignment perched on the edge of the Sahara Desert. All but the White Moors of Mauritania are of the Negroid race, though many, such as the various Fulani peoples, typify the transition zone between Caucasoid Arab North Africa and Negroid sub-Saharan Africa where races have blended together over the centuries.

The West African Muslim complex represents one of the farthest penetrations into the black African interior of the Islamic faith. Most of its peoples are either semi-nomadic, or only recently beginning to adapt to a sedentary lifestyle in the face of the ever-encroaching Sahara Desert.

The challenge of mission to the Sahara, one of the earth's most inhospitable climates, has contributed heavily to the continued dearth of witness among these peoples. Added to the hostile clime is the constant mobility of these desert migrants. The church in the modern age has yet to provide an adequate model for church planting among nomadic peoples.

Fifteen of the largest West African Muslim peoples are identified on the map on page 92. A closer look at one of these peoples, the Hausa of Nigeria, is also provided.

The Hausa of Nigeria

Over 20 million people in Africa call themselves Hausa. Wycliffe's *Ethnologue* reports as many as 25 million Africans speak Hausa as their first or second language. The Hausa people stretch across eighteen nations, from Ethiopia to the Atlantic Ocean, from Algeria in the north to Cameroon in the south.

The largest number of Hausa are in the northern states of Nigeria, where Hausa is the official language. The 18,988,400 Hausa comprise roughly 17% of Nigeria's population. Almost entirely Muslim, they are politically the dominant of Nigeria's four major ethnic populations (the Fulani, Yoruba and Igbo are the other three).

The Hausa translation of the Bible was completed in 1932, and a significant amount of Christian radio broadcasting in this language can be heard in the Hausa territories.

Only about .1% of Nigeria's Hausa are Christians—roughly 19,000 believers. The task for these "quiet believers" to reach their own people is overwhelming. For every Hausa church member, 560 Nigerian Hausa have never heard the gospel of Jesus Christ.

Ethnic and religious hostilities between Muslims and Christians in Nigeria in recent years have made it difficult for Christians living predominantly in the south to share their faith with Hausa neighbors in the north. As a result, nearly 44% of the Hausa people of Nigeria— over ten million Hausa men, women and children—have never heard the gospel of Jesus Christ.

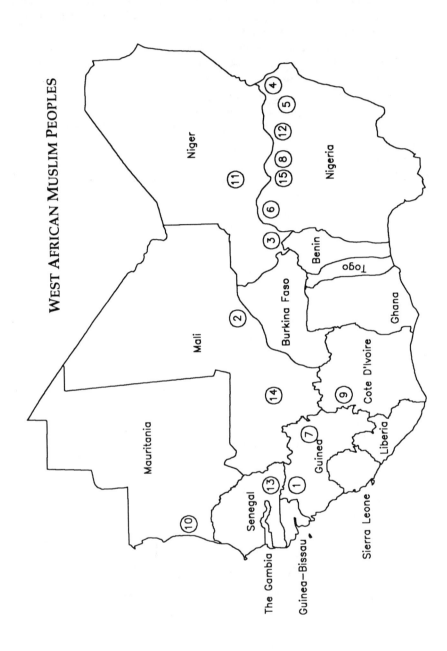

WEST AFRICAN MUSLIM PEOPLES

WEST AFRICAN MUSLIM PEOPLES

No.	People	Country	Language	Pop 1990	Ch affil	Unevang
1	Fula Jalon (Futa Dyalon)	Guinea	Futa Jalo (Pulaar)	1,920,000	200	1,632,000
2	Fula (Peuhala)	Mali	Massina (Fula Peuhala)	835,000	6,300	693,000
3	Zerma (Dyerma)	Niger	Zarma (Dyerma, Adzerma)	1,190,000	100	961,000
4	Kanuri	Nigeria	Kanuri	4,453,000	450	3,607,000
5	Bororo (Western Fulani)	Nigeria	Fulfulde	1,700,000	850	1,322,000
6	Sokoto Fulani	Nigeria	Fulfulde (Sokoto)	1,921,000	2,000	1,441,000
7	Maninka (South Malinke)	Guinea	Maninka (Manding)	1,737,000	17,000	1,285,000
8	Fulani (Haabe)	Nigeria	Fulfulde (Kano-katsina)	1,920,000	7,600	1,402,000
9	Malinke (Ivorian)	Ivory Coast	Maninka (South malinke)	1,390,000	28,000	984,000
10	Bidan (White Moor)	Mauritania	Hassani (Badawi)	1,045,000	20	324,000
11	Hausa (Tazarawa)	Niger	Hausa	1,490,000	150	461,000
12	Fulani (Toroobe)	Nigeria	Hausa (Eastern Hausa)	5,540,000	16,600	3,655,000
13	Fulakunda (Fula Cunda)	Senegal	Fulakunda (Pulaar)	910,000	90	585,000
14	Bambara	Mali	Bamana	2,966,000	119,000	1,869,000
15	Hausa	Nigeria	Hausa	18,990,000	19,000	10,633,000

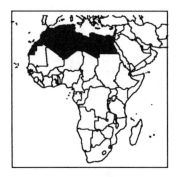

NORTH AFRICAN BERBER PEOPLES

Berbers are a widely dispersed, predominantly Muslim ethnic group of more than 14 million people living in North Africa, the Sahara Desert and Sahelian West Africa. As the earliest identifiable, indigenous ethnic stock in North Africa, Berbers have common cultural traditions, beliefs and legends that set them apart from other peoples, including their various conquerors. All Berbers belong to tribes. Social behavior, life-style, occupations, language and forms of communication, however, differ widely from tribe to tribe and within tribes as well.

Historical developments have led to several distinct Berber languages. There is no common Berber language, and tribal dialects tend towards mutual unintelligibility even within the same country or region. The only dialect in written form is the incomplete Tifinagh script of the Saharan and Sahelian Tuareg.

As an identifiable people, Berbers existed in a state of tribal self-government long before the Arab conquest in the seventh century. The name Berber probably comes from *barbari*, the word meaning "barbarians" applied to them by the Romans. The Berbers do not use the name to describe themselves as a people or ethnic group. The name most commonly used, in slightly different dialectical forms, is *Imazighen*—"free men."

The largest number of Berber groups is in Morocco, where they form about 34% of the population (7.8 million). The Berber proportion in Algeria is about 21.5% (4.5 million). In other countries, the percentages are: Mauritania, 20%; Niger, 8%, Mali, 6%; Libya, 5%. Berbers also form the majority of the population in the sparsely-populated Western Sahara, where they number about 90,000.

Nonresidential missions to the Berbers of North Africa would seek to reach them from a base in France, Belgium or Spain, where large numbers of Berbers reside as laborers. Although it is difficult to make and retain converts within the highly restricted context of North African Muslim cultures, nonresidential missionaries must avoid the temptation to help converts flee North Africa for more congenial lives in Europe or America. North Africa will only see a great movement to Christ when its new believers decide to remain as faithful witnesses in their own context.

Eight of the largest Berber peoples are identified on a map on page 96. The Greater Kabyle of Algeria are profiled in greater detail below.

The Greater Kabyle of Algeria

The third largest group of North African Berbers consists of the nearly 1.9 million Greater Kabyle (Western) Berbers of Algeria. As a result of recent developments, there may be as many as 6,500 Christians among the Kabyle—still less than .4% of their total population.

The Greater Kabyle speak the Qabayil (also called Senhaja or Zwawa) language, which is also understood by 15% of the Algerian populace. Only a New Testament has been translated into the Qabayil language, and this was done in 1901 and is in need of revision. A moderate amount of radio programs are broadcast in Qabayil, both secular and Christian.

As a result of indigenous and external cooperative efforts, there is currently evidence of a significant turning to the gospel among the Kabyle Berber people. Despite this responsiveness, only about 35% of them are evangelized. The majority of this population—well over a million people—have yet to hear the gospel.

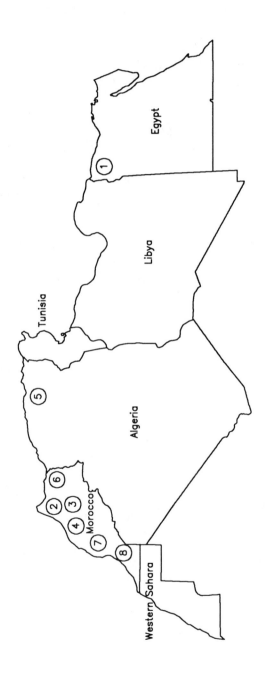

NORTH AFRICAN BERBER PEOPLES

NORTH AFRICAN BERBER PEOPLES

No.	People	Country	Language	Pop 1990	Ch affil	Unevang
1	Arabized Berber	Egypt	Masri (Mashriqi)	1,100,000	1,000	789,000
2	Jebala	Morocco	Maghribi (Mogrebi)	1,080,000	300	735,000
3	Beraber (Tamazight)	Morocco	Tamazight (Beraber, Ksurs)	2,589,000	2,600	1,761,000
4	Arabized Berber	Morocco	Maghribi (Mogrebi)	2,137,000	3,000	1,432,000
5	Greater Kabyle (Western)	Algeria	Qabayil (Senhaja, Zwawa)	1,868,000	6,500	1,214,000
6	Riffian (Northern Shilha)	Morocco	Riff (Senhaja, Iznacen)	1,483,000	2,400	949,000
7	Susiua (Southern Shilha)	Morocco	Susiua (Susi, Susina)	1,006,000	1,000	594,000
8	Shleuh	Morocco	Tachelhait (Masmudah)	1,785,000	2,900	1,053,000

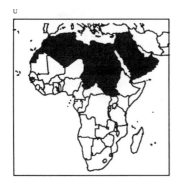

ARABIC PEOPLES

The Arabic complex of peoples live in a stretch of land beginning at the eastern Iraqi border with Iran, and stretching westward to the Atlantic shores of Morocco. Though every group represented in the cluster may not be ethnically Arab, all of them share the Arabic language as their mother tongue. Despite local Arabic variations from one region to another, this unites them in a great communication chain.

The Arabic language is closely linked with the Islamic faith and the conquests that established it across North Africa and the Middle East during the 8th-11th centuries. As one of the world's great languages, Arabic may be studied almost anywhere.

Nonresidential ministries to the Arab world will find tentmaker access easily attainable. The Arab world holds little tolerance for conversion to Christianity, however, heightening the importance of a comprehensive strategy to knit together converts.

Nonresidential ministries to the Arabic-speaking world could be based in Cyprus, where many Middle Eastern ministries are located, or in England and France, where thousands of Arab expatriates live.

Seventeen of the largest Arabic peoples are identified on the map on page 100. A closer look at one of the most influential of the Arabic peoples, the Saudi Arabs of Saudi Arabia, is provided below.

The Saudi Arabs of Saudi Arabia

The Kingdom of Saudi Arabia occupies most of the Arabian peninsula, and is bordered by Jordan, Iraq, Kuwait, the Persian Gulf, Qatar, the United Arab Emirates, Yemen, Oman and the Red Sea. The entire country has a population of just over 11 million. Riyadh is the capital, with Jidda as the principal port, while Mecca and Medina are the chief religious centers.

Though a remarkable degree of modernization has taken place in Saudi Arabia since the discovery of oil in the earlier part of this century, much of the country retains its traditional culture. Thirty percent of the population are still desert-dwelling bedouin. The royal family of ibn Saud rules the country with rigid control.

Two key elements color virtually every aspect of life for the people of Saudi Arabia: religion and petroleum. Two of the holiest Muslim sites are found within the borders of Saudi Arabia, and Islam permeates the society. Almost as pervasive an influence is the existence of more than one-fourth of the world's known reserves of petroleum.

The 9.3 million Saudi Arabs make up nearly two-thirds of Saudi Arabia's population. As a result of their enormous oil wealth, Saudis are among the wealthiest and most powerful people in the world. Their gross national product is more than $100 billion, based almost exclusively on natural petroleum reserves.

Sunni Islam of the wahabi sect is the official religion of Saudi Arabia. While other religions are tolerated within the country, they are severely repressed. Missionaries are strictly forbidden to engage in evangelistic activities. Nonetheless, both the Arabic Bible and Christian radio are available to the Saudi people.

With an estimated literacy rate of less than 50% and tight restrictions on dissemination of Christian literature, Saudi Arabs remain one of the least evangelized people in this region of the world.

Less than .1% of the Saudi Arab people—perhaps 8,400 individuals—claim Christianity as their religion, and the majority of these must keep their faith secret. This leaves more than nine million who have no professed relationship with God through Jesus Christ. Research indicates that as many as 58% of the Saudi Arab people—five million people—have never heard about the claims of Jesus Christ.

ARABIC PEOPLES

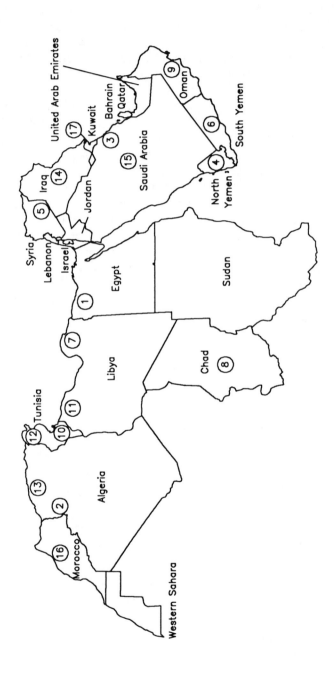

ARABIC PEOPLES

No.	People	Country	Language	Pop 1990	Ch affil	Unevang
1	Bedouin	Egypt	Badawi (Bedouin Arabic)	1,081,000	20	865,000
2	Hamyan Bedouin	Algeria	Badawi (Bedouin Arabic)	1,770,000	150	1,381,000
3	Yemeni Arab	Saudi Arabia	Arabiya (Saudi Arabic)	2,968,000	600	2,107,000
4	Yemeni Arab North	Yemen	Arabiya (Yemeni Arabic)	7,767,000	750	5,437,000
5	Bedouin Arab	Syria	Badawi (Bedouin Arabic)	950,000	100	638,000
6	Yemeni Arab	South Yemen	Arabiya (Yemeni Arabic)	2,059,000	800	1,421,000
7	Cyrenaican Arab	Libya	Barqi (Mashriqi)	1,182,000	200	804,000
8	Chad Arab	Chad	Arabiya (Chad Arabic)	1,455,000	1,500	975,000
9	Omani Arab	Oman	Arabiya (Omani Arabic)	1,057,000	1,100	708,000
10	Sahel Bedouin	Tunisia	Badawi (Bedouin Arabic)	1,748,000	1,700	1,171,000
11	Tripolitanian Arab	Libya	Tarabulusi (Maghribi)	1,364,000	300	900,000
12	Tunisian Arab	Tunisia	Ifriqi (Maghribi)	5,464,000	8,200	3,606,000
13	Algerian Arab	Algeria	Jazairi (Maghribi)	17,701,000	53,100	11,329,000
14	Iraqi Arab	Iraq	Arabiya (Iraqi Arabic)	12,944,000	91,000	8,155,000
15	Saudi Arab	Saudi Arabia	Arabiya (Saudi Arabic)	9,292,000	8,400	5,389,000
16	Moroccan Arab	Morocco	Maghribi (Mogrebi)	12,595,000	19,000	6,549,000
17	Kuwaiti Arab	Kuwait	Arabiya (Kuwait Arabic)	870,000	22,600	435,000

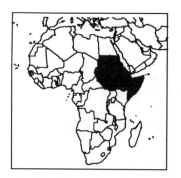

EAST AFRICAN CUSHITIC PEOPLES

The East African Cushitic cluster of peoples live in southern Egypt, Sudan, Ethiopia and Somalia. Their name comes from the Biblical designation for the peoples of the region beyond upper Egypt. Though Arabic is widely spoken among the Cushites of this region, indigenous languages reveal a common linguistic link to a more basic Cushitic language family.

Famine and a hostile climate have taken a heavy toll on the Cushites. As a result of these rigorous conditions, the land is sparsely populated. Many of the people are nomads and pursue seasonal water and pastures.

About 20 million unevangelized Cushites are scattered throughout this region. The largest of these are the more than eight million Somali of Somalia and Ethiopia. Two of the peoples included in this complex, the Bor-Agar and Rek Dinka peoples, are Negro, and not of the Cushitic race. Their location, religious faith and lifestyle, however, place them within the aegis of the Cushitic world.

Given their ethnic, linguistic and geographic position between the Arabic and Negro worlds, a nonresidential ministry to the Cushitic peoples could tap resources from both arenas. Nonresidential missionaries would seek to draw Arabic resources, such as those clustered in Cyprus and Egypt, farther south into Sudan. They would also try to challenge some of the hundreds of Christian mission agencies in such key African centers as Nairobi, Kenya, to press north into the regions of the Cushitic world.

Eight of the largest Cushitic peoples are located on the map on page 104. A closer look at the least evangelized of these peoples, the Beja of the Sudan, is also provided.

The Beja or Beni-Amer of Sudan

The Sudan is the largest country on the African continent in terms of square miles. Nearly eight percent, or 1.2 million of Sudan's 25 million people, call themselves Beja or the Beni-Amer. They live along the steep slopes of the Red Sea Hills overlooking a narrow coastal plain 10-25 miles wide and festooned with dunes and coral reefs. Their population stretches south into the Eritrean region of Ethiopia, where a further 39,000 Beja live.

Historically, the Beja are a semi-nomadic people, Cushitic in origin like the Ethiopians and Somali. The precise proportion of nomads in the Beja population today is not known, but it is far greater than the percentage of nomads among the Arab population.

Most Beja belong to one of four tribal groups. The largest of these is the Hadendowa, some of whom are engaged in agriculture in the coastal regions of Kassala near Tokar. Others are nomads. The Bisharin tribal group occupies the most land, with tribes settled on the Atbara River, south of the Beja range, and nomads living in the north. The Amarar, who live in the central part of the Beja range, seem to be largely nomads, as are the second largest group, the Beni-Amir, who live along the border near northern Ethiopia.

The Beja tend to be indifferent to trade and modernization, and have been reluctant to accept the authority of central governments. This resistance to outside influences makes serving the Beja in the name of Jesus difficult.

In the sixth century, most Beja were Christian, but since the 13th century, most have been Muslim. Today, the Beja are one of the peoples in Africa with the least exposure to Christianity. Research has failed to uncover a single Beja believer. Despite efforts at producing a Bible, Wycliffe Bible Translators reports no Scripture for these people. More than one Scripture translation will probably be needed to reach them. The best estimates are that more than 90% of the Beja—over one million people—have never heard the gospel of Jesus Christ.

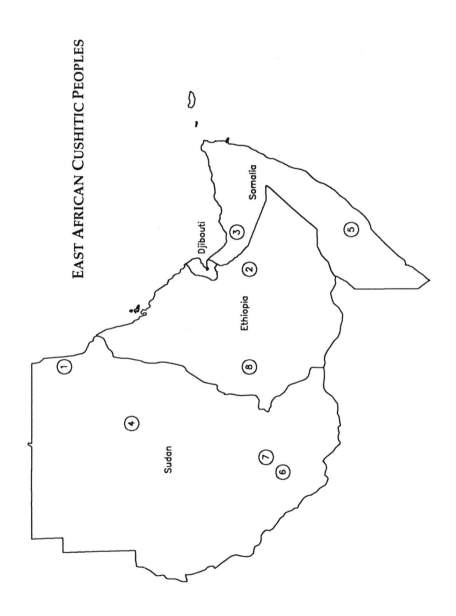

EAST AFRICAN CUSHITIC PEOPLES

EAST AFRICAN CUSHITIC PEOPLES

No.	People	Country	Language	Pop 1990	Ch affil	Unevang
1	Beja (Beni-Amer, Ababda)	Sudan	Bedawye (Beja, Bedawiya)	1,160,000	1	1,067,000
2	Somali	Ethiopia	Somali (Soomaali)	2,452,000	250	2,011,000
3	Sab	Somalia	Somali (Sab)	816,000	20	637,000
4	Gaaliin	Sudan	Ja'ali (Mashriqi-badawi)	1,687,000	24,000	1,232,000
5	Somali	Somalia	Somali (Somalinya)	5,940,000	2,400	4,158,000
6	Bor-Agar (East Central Dinka)	Sudan	Jieng (Bor-agar Denka)	1,007,0000	83,000	675,000
7	Rek (Western) Dinka	Sudan	Jieng (Rek Dinka)	905,000	72,000	461,000
8	Arusi Galla (Oromo)	Ethiopia	Arusi (Arsi, Oromo)	2,647,000	79,000	1,297,000

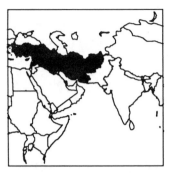

KURDO-IRANIAN PEOPLES

The Kurdo-Iranian population complex stretches from the mountains of Eastern Turkey to the borders of Southwest China, and includes peoples as diverse as the Kurds and the Tadzhiks. What this complex holds in common are Indo-European origin and linguistic affinity. There are some exceptions to this common ethnic heritage, like the Hazara Berberi of Afghanistan, who are actually Mongolian remnants of Genghis Khan's armies of the 13th century. Though their Mongolian racial characteristics remain unchanged, their use of the Dari trade language and practice of Shiite religion place them within the orbit of the Kurdo-Iranian world.

Virtually all of the Kurdo-Iranian peoples are Muslim, though some are Sunni, while others are Shiite. Throughout the Kurdo-Iranian world, there is a dynamic and often hostile tension with the great Turkic complex of peoples.

Nonresidential missionaries serving any of the peoples or cities in the Kurdo-Iranian complex could share models of ministry, and even share translators for the production of Scripture, Christian literature and radio broadcasting.

Eighteen of the largest Kurdo-Iranian peoples are identified on the map on page 108. A more detailed look at one of these peoples, the Iranian or Farsi-Speaking Kurds of Iran, is also provided.

The Iranian or Farsi-Speaking Kurds of Iran

Population figures for the total number of Kurds worldwide varies considerably from eight to 20 million. It is difficult to determine an exact figure because of numerous social, geographical and political reasons. Large concentrations of Kurds live in Turkey, Iraq, Syria, West Germany, USSR, Kuwait, Lebanon, Netherlands and France, as well as Iran. The majority of Kurds today live in the strategic gulf region between Europe and the Soviet Union called "Kurdistan." Kurdistan is located where the borders of Iraq, Iran, Turkey and Syria meet.

In Iran, the Kurdish community exceeds eight million, nearly 20% of the country's total population. At least five different Kurdish language communities or peoples live in Iran: the Sorani-, Kurmanji-, Mukri- and Farsi-speaking Kurds.

The largest group are the 2.6 million Iranian, or Farsi-speaking Kurds. Living along the Zagros mountain range of western Iran, the

Kurds comprise roughly six percent of Iran's total population. Historically, the Kurds have been a mountain people living in a region which, until recent history, has been beyond the reach of governments, and is known as the "land of insolence."

The Kurds are most probably the descendants of the Medes of the seventh and sixth centuries B.C. Several Kurds have been prominent in history: Darius, the Medean king of Persia at the time of Daniel, and Saladin, one of Islam's great defenders during the times of the Crusades.

Farsi-speaking Kurds have had access to Scripture in their mother tongue since 1838, when the first Farsi translation was completed. Less than 43% of Iran's adult population is literate, however, and among the Kurds, this figure is probably higher. Because of this, radio broadcasting is of great significance in communicating to Iranian Kurds. A significant amount of radio broadcasting in Farsi is currently received in Iran.

Despite this and other efforts, few Kurdish responses to the gospel have been registered. Research reveals no more than 800 Iranian Kurdish believers—less than .03% of the entire Iranian Kurdish population. As many as 74% of the entire Iranian Kurdish population— nearly two million people—have yet to hear the gospel of Jesus Christ.

More than five million Iranians have fled Iran since the 1979 Islamic revolution. A nonresidential ministry to the Kurdish people could be based in any of the numerous Kurdish expatriate populations of Western Europe and the United States. When considering the prospects of influencing change among Iranian Kurds from a base in Europe, we can recall that the Ayatollah Khomeini's successful revolution in Iran during the decade of the seventies was engineered outside the country.

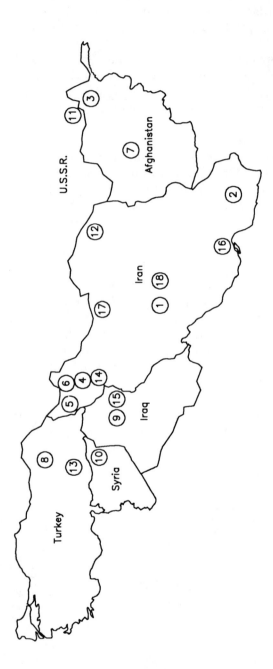

KURDO-IRANIAN PEOPLES

KURDO-IRANIAN PEOPLES

No.	People	Country	Language	Pop 1990	Ch affil	Unevang
1	Bakhtiari	Iran	Bakhtiari (Luri)	1,080,000	20	978,000
2	Baluchi	Iran	Baluchi	1,245,000	10	1,108,000
3	Tadzhik	Afghanistan	Tadzhik (Galcha, Dari)	3,924,000	10	3,414,000
4	Gilaki	Iran	Gilaki (Gelaki, Gilani)	3,282,000	10	2,823,000
5	Central Kurd	Iran	Mukri (Eastern Kermanji)	1,132,000	300	974,000
6	Southern Kurd Carduchi	Iran	Kermanshahi (Kurdi)	2,829,000	1,400	2,433,000
7	Hazara (Berberi)	Afghanistan	Hazaragi (Afghan Persian)	1,060,000	500	890,000
8	Northern Kurd (Kermanji)	Turkey	Zaza (Dimli, Gurmanji)	5,005,000	500	4,154,000
9	Northern Kurd	Iraq	Kermanji (Hakari, Jezire)	2,820,000	2,000	2,341,000
10	Western Kurd (Kermanji)	Syria	Kermanji (Kurdi)	958,000	1,200	795,000
11	Tadzhik	Soviet Union	Tadzhik	3,184,000	300	2,611,000
12	Afghan Persian Kaboli	Iran	Dari (Kaboli, Khorasani)	1,580,000	800	1,299,000
13	Turkish Kurd	Turkey	Turkce (Turkish)	4,450,000	450	3,293,000
14	Iranian Kurd	Iran	Farsi (Persian)	3,395,000	1,000	2,512,000
15	Iraqi Kurd	Iraq	Arabiya (Iraqi Arabic)	1,140,000	600	817,000
16	Luri (Lori)	Iran	Luri (Feyli, Alaki, Kelhuri)	3,225,000	10	2,258,000
17	Mazanderani	Iran	Mazanderani (Tabri, Palari)	2,603,000	10	1,744,000
18	Persian (Irani)	Iran	Farsi (Persian, Dari)	18,903,000	7,600	8,884,000

TURKIC PEOPLES

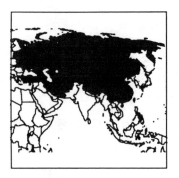

The Turkic population complex occupies the region known as Turkestan—"Land of the Turks"—stretching from the Anatolian peninsula of Turkey to the Mongolian border of China's Xinjiang Province. Large numbers live in the Soviet Union, Turkey, China, Afghanistan and Iran. Though a number of diverse languages are spoken across Turkestan, they all belong to the Turkic family of languages. Consequently, Christians serving one of the Turkic peoples will find it possible to transfer into an adjacent Turkic assignment if it becomes necessary to move.

Nonresidential missionaries will quickly realize that the geographic, politcal, and cultural insulation of the region is one of the main reasons why the Turkic peoples have been without Christ for so long. As Soviet policies of *glasnost* and *perestroika* increasingly open the Soviet Union to the outside world, opportunities for Christian witness to this remote region will increase.

A nonresidential ministry to this region could have its base in Western Europe. West Germany, in particular, has a large number of expatriates from Soviet Turkestan and the nation of Turkey living within its borders.

Fourteen of the least evangelized Turkic peoples are located on the map on page 112. One of the largest and most influential, the Uzbek of the USSR, is profiled in some detail.

The Uzbek of the USSR

The great majority of the world's nearly 20 million Uzbek people live in the Soviet republic that bears their name. The Uzbek Soviet Socialist Republic is also known as Uzbekstan, or "Land of the Uzbek." An additional 877,000 live across the border in Afghanistan, and a few thousand in the neighboring countries of China and Mongolia.

The Uzbek are a Turko-Mongolian people, tracing their ancestry back to the great population migrations of Genghis Khan and the Gold Horde of Tamerlane in the 13th-15th centuries. In the USSR, the Uzbek are the largest non-European ethnic group and the third largest Soviet nationality.

From the days of the Timurid dynasty of the 14th-15th centuries, the Uzbek cities of Tashkent, Samarkand and Bukhara were reknowned as educational and trade centers. Each year, students in the thousands came from many parts of the Muslim East to attend the seminaries. Though Uzbekstan is effectively separated from the non-Soviet Muslim world, it remains a significant center of Central Asian Islamic thought and culture.

More than 77% of the Uzbeks still live in rural areas. Russians, Tatars, Ukranians, Jews and Armenians make up much of Uzbekstan's urban population, as peoples from the western Soviet Republics move east to the cities of Uzbekstan. The capital of Uzbekstan, Tashkent—with a population of 2.4 million—is Central Asia's largest city, and the fourth largest city in the Soviet Union. Samarkand is the second largest Uzbek city and the oldest, dating back 2,500 years.

Uzbeks are almost exclusively Hanafi Sunni, or orthodox Sunni, although the most vibrant expression of Islam in the region is a mystical Sufism, which has kept Islam alive in the midst of anti-religious pressures from Moscow. Anthropologists also point to the survival of many Shamanistic religious practices from the pre-Islamic religion of the region. While there may be as many as a few hundred Uzbek Christians, most have had to keep their faith hidden to avoid social repercussions.

Some Christian radio broadcasting in the Uzbek language is transmitted into Central Asia. Portions of the Bible were translated into Uzbek in the late 19th century, but this text is now unintelligible to modern-day Uzbeks. A new translation project is underway, but has not yet been completed for publication or distribution.

For generations, Communist and Islamic barriers have hindered the evangelization of the Uzbek people. Research indicates that as many as 7.5 million Uzbek living in the USSR have never heard about the love of Christ.

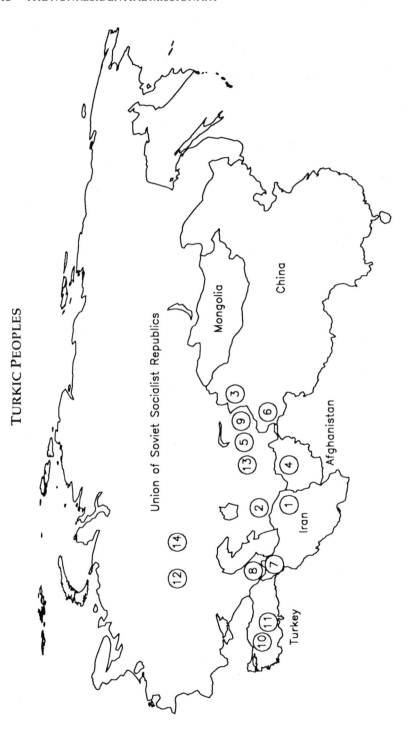

TURKIC PEOPLES

TURKIC PEOPLES

No.	People	Country	Language	Pop 1990	Ch affil	Unevang
1	Turkmen (Turkomani)	Iran	Turkmen (Anauli, Esari, Teke)	910,000	20	833,000
2	Turkmen	Soviet Union	Turkmen (Jagarta)	2,228,000	10	1,961,000
3	Kazakh	China	Hasaka (Kazakh)	927,000	10	779,000
4	Uzbek	Afghanistan	Uzbek (Kypchak)	880,000	90	738,000
5	Kirghiz	Soviet Union	Kirghiz (Kara, Black)	2,094,000	400	1,738,000
6	Uighur (Kashgar)	China	Wei wuer (I-kha, Lop)	6,709,000	30	5,434,000
7	Azerbaijani (Turk)	Iran	Azeri (Tabris, Moqaddan)	7,158,000	40	5,655,000
8	Azerbaijani (Azurbijan)	Soviet Union	Azeri (Azerbaijani)	6,018,000	50	4,574,000
9	Kazakh	Soviet Union	Kazakh (Western Kirghiz)	7,204,000	720	5,403,000
10	Crimean Tatar	Turkey	Turkce (Turkish)	3,893,000	400	2,842,000
11	Turk	Turkey	Turkce (Turkish)	38,669,000	7,700	26,682,000
12	Tatar (Kazan Tatar)	Soviet Union	Kazan Tatar	6,941,000	104,000	3,471,000
13	Uzbek	Soviet Union	Uzbek	17,687,000	1,300	8,313,000
14	Bashkir	Soviet Union	Bashkir (Bashkirian)	1,506,000	109,000	542,000

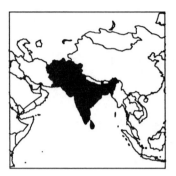

SOUTH ASIAN MUSLIM PEOPLES

The South Asian Muslim complex of peoples includes the Islamic populations of five South Asian nations: India, Bangladesh, Pakistan, Sri Lanka and parts of Afghanistan.

While some would contest the inclusion of Afghanistan in this collection, Afghanistan is a transitional or buffer state between the Kurdo-Iranian complex, the Turkic complex and the South Asian complex of peoples. In this regard, it is somewhat like Switzerland, which consists of Italian, French and German sectors. As a buffer state between civilizations, Afghanistan's population consists of Turkic, Iranian and South Asian Muslim peoples.

The diverse South Asian people cluster is united by an allegiance to the Islamic faith, and by the trade and travel links that have emerged from this bond.

All nonresidential missionaries serving any of the South Asian Muslim peoples would need to rely on Christians with experience in sharing the gospel with Muslims. They would also need to tailor their message to the distinctives of Islamic culture as it has evolved under the various civilizations of the Indian subcontinent and surrounding lands.

While residence within some of the South Asian countries is possible for short periods of time, a nonresidential missionary would ultimately find it necessary to tap into the greater concentration of Christian resources available from a base in Singapore or even London.

Twelve of the largest South Asian Muslim peoples are identified on the map on page 116. A closer look at a South Asian Muslim people, the Deccani of India, is also provided.

The Deccani of India

The Deccan plateau in Central India coincides with what used to be the princely state of Maharashtra, which was ruled until 1948 by a Sunni Muslim dynasty, the Asaf Jahs, descendants of the great Mughals of India. The plateau's Muslim inhabitants, now citizens of the state of Andra Pradesh, Mysore and Maharashtra, number 11.8 million, and share to a great extent a distinctive heritage and culture.

Muslims have always been a small minority of the population of Deccan—never more than 12%—yet for nearly five centuries they ruled the region. Since its very beginning, Muslim rule in the Deccan largely depended on the immigration of Muslims from other Islamic countries. In 1948, the newly independent government of India forcibly deposed the Muslim dynasty of Asaf Jahs. This event had a significant effect on the political, cultural and socio-economic condition of the Deccani Muslims. Millions immigrated to Pakistan. Those who remained faced the necessity of adjusting to radically changed circumstances.

There are no more than 100 known Deccani Christians. This leaves a ratio of more than 56,000 Deccani people who have never responded to the gospel to each Deccani believer, making them one of the least evangelized groups in India. Despite the existence of numerous Christians in the states of Andra Pradesh and Maharashtra, where most Deccani live, there is little Christian work among the Deccani people. This is due in large part to the social tensions between Muslims and the rest of Indian society.

The Deccani language, Dakhini or Hyderabadi Urdu, is different enough from Urdu to separate the Deccani from other Urdu speakers and bind them together as a people, yet this difference also keeps them isolated from Urdu ministries. No Christian radio program broadcasts specifically for the Deccani people. The Dakhini New Testament was translated in 1758, but due to the evolution of the language, it is virtually useless today.

As a result of their relative proximity to Christians, about half of the Deccani have heard the gospel of Jesus Christ. Nonetheless, research reveals few converts. It is estimated that nearly six million Deccani men, women and children have no knowledge of the gospel.

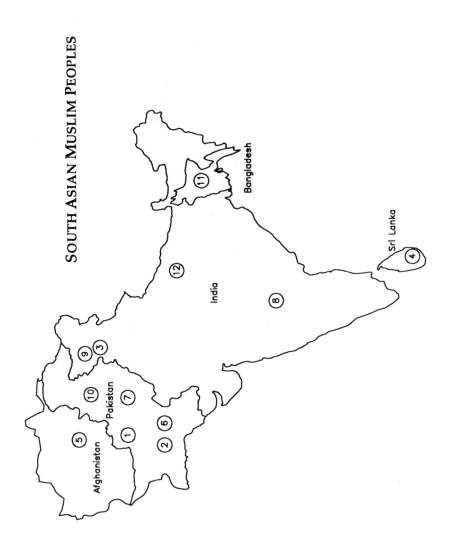

SOUTH ASIAN MUSLIM PEOPLES

SOUTH ASIAN MUSLIM PEOPLES

No.	People	Country	Language	Pop 1990	Ch affil	Unevang
1	Brahui	Pakistan	Brahui	910,000	1,800	782,000
2	Baluchi	Pakistan	Baluchi	3,671,000	20	3,120,000
3	Dogri	India	Dogri (Dhogaryali, Bhatholi)	1,850,000	1,900	1,408,000
4	Ceylon Moor	Sri Lanka	Tamil	1,120,000	20	820,000
5	Pathan (Pushtun, Afghani)	Afghanistan	Passhto (Pushtu, Pakhtu)	8,617,000	1,700	6,032,000
6	Sindhi	Pakistan	Sindhi (Lari, Lasi)	17,808,000	1,800	10,685,000
7	Urdu	Pakistan	Urdu	11,160,000	1,100	6,584,000
8	Deccani (Dakhini Hindi)	India	Dakhini (Hyderabadi Urdu)	11,790,000	100	6,247,000
9	Kashmiri (Keshur)	India	Kashmiri (Poguli, Rambani)	3,772,000	750	1,773,000
10	Pathan (Afghani, Waziri)	Pakistan	Pashto (Pushtu, Paktu)	12,480,000	1,000	5,867,000
11	Bihari (Urdu-speaking)	Bangladesh	Urdu	1,734,000	170	728,000
12	Urdu (Islami, Undri, Urudu)	India	Urdu	44,542,000	4,500	13,808,000

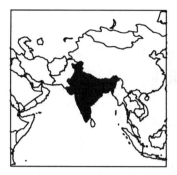

SOUTH ASIAN HINDUSTANI PEOPLES

The South Asian Hindustani population complex is massive, and includes much of the population of India and the Himalayan nations of Nepal, Bhutan and Sikkim, as well as parts of Sri Lanka and Bangladesh. The term Hindustani refers to those peoples which live in the "Place of the Hindu"—Hindu referring not only the practitioners of the Hindu religion, but all of those religions which have long found their home under the influence of Indian culture.

In terms of religious practice, South Asia is one of the most diverse on earth. The peoples within the Hindustani complex largely adhere to various expressions of Hinduism and tribal religions, though Sikkhism, Buddhism and Jainism are also in evidence.

The diverse peoples within the complex are united by residence in the South Asian subcontinent. Correspondingly, nonresidential missions to peoples or cities in this complex must share resources to serve these peoples. They must also cooperate closely with the growing number of evangelical churches and mission agencies in southern India, encouraging and helping them to take their unrestricted witness into the unevangelized regions of the north.

Expatriate nonresidential missionaries will find it relatively easy to spend a few months in either India or Nepal for language study and cultural orientation. Both nations, however, are opposed to evangelistic missionary work by foreigners.

Twenty of the largest and least evangelized South Asian Hindustani peoples are identified on the map on page 120. It is significant to note that virtually all of them are located north of the southern one-quarter of the Indian subcontinent. It is in this southern quarter that Christianity is most pervasive. A closer look at one of the unevangelized peoples in the complex, the Central Bhil of India, is also provided.

The Central Bhil of India

More than 6.7 million Bhil people live in western India, and can be subdivided into three major distinct population segments: the Eastern Bhil (or Vil), with 2,154,900 people; the Central Bhil, with 3,582,400 people; and the Southern Bhil, with 1,014,400 people. Most Bhil live in the border region connecting the states of Gujarat and Rajasthan.

According to *Ethnologue*, smaller numbers of Bhil also live in Andra Pradesh, Madhya Pradesh, Bihar, Jammu, Kashmir, Maharashtra, Karnataka, Punjab, and Rajasthan.

In contrast to the two major racial stocks of India, the Aryan and Dravidian, the Bhil appear to be pre-Aryan and pre-Dravidian in origin, related to the aboriginal Austro-Asiatic races of people. While the majority of them are tribal religionists and do not practice higher Hinduism, some have been assimilated into Hindu castes in urban areas. Only the Tadavi Bhil (those speaking the Tadavi language) are predominantly Muslim.

The name "Bhil" has come to refer to the ethnic designation to which these people belong, but appears to be linked etymologically to the local word for "bow" (as in bow and arrow), indicating the warlike legacy of the Bhil. Other names for the Bhil are Bhili, Bhilbari, Bhilla, and Vil.

The 3.6 million Central Bhil may have as many as 11,000 church members, roughly .3% of their population. The language of the Central Bhil is called Bhili or Bhilori, though many are bilingual, speaking the local language of the district in which they live.

Only a portion of the New Testament has been translated into the Bhili language. This portion is called the *Bhili: Central Bible*, and was completed in 1916. There is currently no radio broadcasting, secular or religious, in the Bhili language.

The Central Bhil are one of the least evangelized peoples in India. Research indicates that no more than 18% of the Central Bhil people have heard the gospel, leaving about three million Central Bhil with no access to the good news of Jesus Christ.

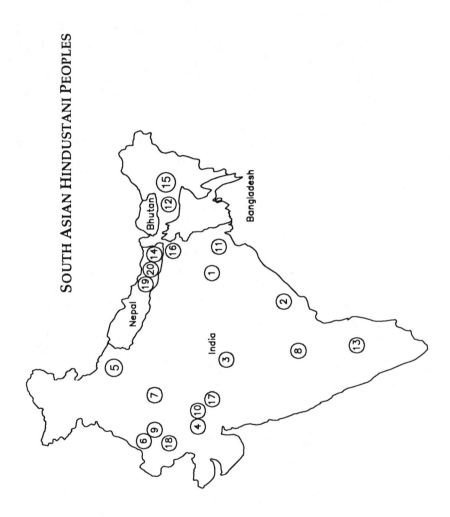

SOUTH ASIAN HINDUSTANI PEOPLES

SOUTH ASIAN HINDUSTANI PEOPLES

No.	People	Country	Language	Pop 1990	Ch affil	Unevang
1	Nagpuri Bihari (Sadri)	India	Sadan (Nagpuri, Dikkukaji)	1,900,000	380	1,633,000
2	Gond (North and Central)	India	Mandla Gondi (Betul, Gondu)	2,560,000	850	2,176,000
3	Nimadi (Nimari)	India	Nimadi (Nemadi, Bhuani)	1,240,000	1,200	1,052,000
4	Wagdi (Wagheri, Vagdi, Vaged)	India	Wagdi (Vagi, Wagholi)	1,472,000	1,500	1,251,000
5	Garhwali (Central Pahari)	India	Tehri	853,000	250	717,000
6	Bagri (Bahgri)	India	Bagri (Baorias)	1,644,000	1,600	1,381,000
7	Mina	India	Mina	2,244,000	6,700	1,885,000
8	Lamani (Banjara, Labhani)	India	Lamani (Lambadi, Kora)	1,874,000	2,400	1,555,000
9	Rajasthani	India	Bikaneri, Mewari	1,707,000	1,900	1,400,000
10	Bhil (Central, East and Southern)	India	Bhili, Dehwali, Valvi	7,431,000	18,700	5,945,000
11	Ho	India	Ho (Lanka Kol, Lohara)	1,168,000	6,400	946,000
12	Kumaoni (Central Pahari)	India	Kumuni (Kumgoni)	1,923,000	7,700	1,538,000
13	Tulu (Tullu, Thulu, Tal)	India	Tulu (Tilu, Tuluva Bhasa)	1,802,000	18,000	1,370,000
14	Tamang (Tamar, Sain)	Nepal	Tamang	946,000	470	719,000
15	Manipuri (Methei, Kathe)	India	Manipuri (Ponna)	1,216,000	13,000	876,000
16	Nepalese (Gurkhali)	India	Khas Kura (Nepali, Palpa)	2,004,000	800	1,423,000
17	Malvi (Ujjaini, Malavi)	India	Malvi (Bachadi, Patvi)	1,003,000	90,000	311,000
18	Sindhi (Kachchi, Bhatia)	India	Sindhi (Lari, Thareli)	1,876,000	21,000	1,277,000
19	Bhojpuri Bihari	Nepal	Bhojpuri	1,375,000	300	880,000
20	Maitili (Tirahutia)	Nepal	Maitili	2,262,000	4,500	1,425,000

NORTHERN CHINA PEOPLES

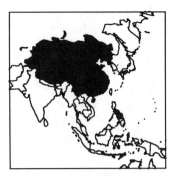

The Northern China cluster of peoples extends beyond the bounds of China to include North Korea and Mongolia, since northern China's influence extends over these two bordering nations. Historically, Mongolia and North Korea have had their plight intertwined with that of China. Even today, nearly two million Koreans live in China, and more Mongolians live in China than in the entire nation of Mongolia.

Although there is less ethnic diversity in the Northern China complex of peoples than in most of the other twelve complexes, the massive number of 744 million Mandarin Chinese render it the most populous of all the world's unevangelized clusters of people. With the exception of Mongolia, the remainder of the Northern China region is one of the most densely populated on earth. Over half of the world's least evangelized cities are located in this territory.

As the gateway to China, Hong Kong continues to provide a key base of residence for anyone considering a nonresidential ministry to the Northern China population complex. As the countries of the Northern China complex continue to extend their relations to the outside world, however, other Asian cities such as Tokyo, Seoul and Taipei also offer excellent settings for a nonresidential ministry.

Seven of the largest Northern China peoples are identified on the map on page 124. A detailed look at one of the Manchu is also provided.

The Manchu of China

Nearly five million Manchu live in the northeastern Chinese provinces of Heilongjiang, Jilin, and Liaoning (formerly Manchuria) as well as in Beijing. Manchuria consists primarily of forested hills, mountains, fertile plains and semi-arid grasslands. Various distinct cultural patterns have emerged in these different environments, and its rich resources have attracted migrations from eastern Siberia, the Mongolian plateau, the Korean peninsula and China.

Research indicates that the Juchen-Manchu are members of a widespread ethnic group known as the Tungus. The Manchu, like all the other Tungus peoples, are related to the Turko-Mongolian races, but they have interbred widely with other peoples, especially Han Chinese to the south.

In the 19th and 20th centuries, as widespread political unrest shook China, Manchuria grew tremendously. In the years preceding World War II, the Japanese invaded Manchuria and incorporated it as the colony of "Manchukuo." From this base of operations, they imported Japanese colonialists and expanded further into China, setting up a government under a puppet emperor of Manchu heritage.

With the defeat of the Japanese in 1945 came an end to the Japanese colony of Manchukuo. In 1949, all land in Manchuria was divided among the peasants. Today, the Japanese have returned to Manchuria as major developers of industry and purchasers of raw materials mined in the area.

Because they ruled China for nearly 300 years, the Manchu have suffered some retribution from the Han Chinese. Consequently, literature and communication in the Manchu has gradually fallen into disuse. A New Testament was first published in the Manchu language, also called Sibo or Juchen, in 1835. This Manchu New Testament is unavailable today. Little literature is published and no broadcasting is done either inside or outside China in the Manchu language.

The religious practices of the Manchu are divided between traditional Chinese folk religion, Buddhism, Siberian shamanism and some atheism. Roughly 86% of the Manchu—more than 4 million people—have never had the opportunity to respond to the gospel of Jesus Christ.

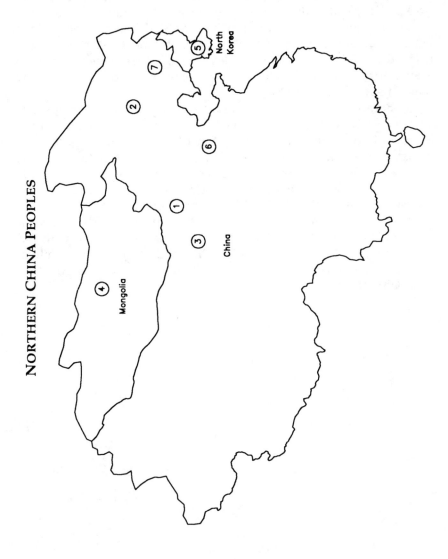

NORTHERN CHINA PEOPLES

No.	People	Country	Language	Pop 1990	Ch affil	Unevang
1	Khalka Mongol (Mongolian)	China	Khalka (Dariganga, Urat)	3,840,000	800	3,343,000
2	Manchu	China	Sibo (Manchu, Juchen)	4,840,000	1,000	4,164,000
3	Hui (Dungan, Tunya)	China	Kuoyu (Mandarin)	8,130,000	20	6,017,000
4	Khalka Mongol	Mongolia	Khalka (Mongolian)	1,480,000	400	1,083,000
5	Korean	North Korea	Chosenmal (Korean)	22,720,000	207,000	15,675,000
6	Han Chinese (Mandarin)	China	Putonghua (Standard)	744,905,000	30,361,000	372,453,000
7	Korean	China	Chaoxian (Korean)	1,986,000	119,000	943,000

SOUTHERN CHINA PEOPLES

Peoples in the Southern China population complex live below the Yangtze River, which empties into the Pacific Ocean at the great city of Shanghai, and then winds its way westward to Chengdu, the capital city of Szechuan Province. Southern China includes peoples as diverse as the Tibetans, Zhuang and Cantonese. While the greatest number of these peoples are non-Chinese ethnic minorities, the complex includes tens of millions of ethnic Han Chinese.

As the Peoples Republic of China continues to exert its centralized control over the regions of the country remote from Beijing, there will be a growing capability of Chinese Christians to evangelize this region. At present, however, limitations of Chinese freedom to travel, do research on, and evangelize these outlying provinces highlights the continued importance of missionary and tentmaker contributions from foreigners.

Hong Kong continues to be a strategic center for nonresidential missionary and other Christian ministries aimed at the China mainland. As China's trade with other Asian nations increases, however, new centers emerge such as Taipei, Tokyo and Singapore.

Fifteen of the largest and least evangelized Southern China peoples are identified on the map on page 128. A sample look at one of the largest and least evangelized non-Chinese peoples from this complex, the Zhuang of China, is also provided.

The Zhuang of China

The Zhuang people of China have a rapidly growing population of more than 15 million, roughly equivalent to that of Australia. They are the largest non-Chinese nationality in the People's Republic of China.

The Zhuang live predominantly on the plains and the river valleys in the mountainous western portions of Guangxi Province in southern China, west of Hong Kong and just north of Vietnam. They are largely subsistence farmers, cultivating wet rice in paddy fields. These Zhuang are often called "water dwellers" because their settlements are close to water and their dwellings are constructed on piles or stilts. Their practices easily merge with that of the Chinese.

In contrast, Zhuang who live in the mountainous regions follow their own social customs and have a definite sense of ethnic identity.

The majority of Zhuang have inhabited Guangxi since classical antiquity. For two millennia, they have coexisted with the Chinese. In the early 20th century, Guangxi became the base of Sun Yat-sen's nationalist revolution. Between 1927 and 1931, the Zhuang formed a string of elected Communist organizational units that gave rise to new Communist leaders.

Their religion is a mixture of Buddhism and animism, and they worship the spirits of their ancestors. Any and all of the restrictions on Christian work in China also apply on efforts to serve this segment of the population.

Recently, Christian radio broadcasts to the Zhuang have begun, and a translation of the Zhuang Bible has been initiated. At present, however, the Zhuang remain the largest language community in the world with no Scripture or other Christian literature in their own language.

As a result of a recent increase in the level of Christian witness to the Zhuang people, a number of Zhuang people have converted. Early efforts reveal that the Zhuang are a highly responsive people when they have an opportunity to hear the gospel. Research indicates, however, that more than 10 million Zhuang men, women and children have yet to hear the gospel of Jesus Christ.

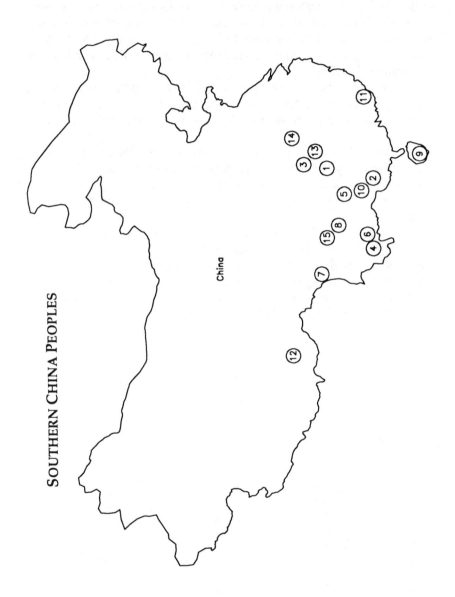

SOUTHERN CHINA PEOPLES

China

SOUTHERN CHINA PEOPLES

No.	People	Country	Language	Pop 1990	Ch affil	Unevang
1	Tung (Dong, Kam)	China	Kam (Tung-chia, Tong)	1,610,000	1,600	1,396,000
2	Zhuang (Chuang, Chwang)	China	Chwang (Chuang, Yungpei)	15,070,000	30,000	12,958,000
3	Tujia (Tuchia)	China	Tuchia	3,191,000	13,000	2,744,000
4	I (Yi, Lolo)	China	Nesu (Lolo, I, Yi)	6,140,000	6,000	5,221,000
5	Meo (North, East, West)	China	Miao, Meo	6,667,000	24,000	4,760,000
6	Hani	China	Hani (Woni, Ho, Haw)	1,190,000	48,000	977,000
7	Bai (Pai, Minchia)	China	Pai (Minchia, Minkia)	1,270,000	25,000	1,032,000
8	Puyi (Bouyei, Pu-I)	China	Chungchia (Dioi, Jui)	2,388,000	24,000	1,934,000
9	Han Chinese (Hainanese)	China	Wanning (Wenchang)	5,109,731	20,000	4,139,000
10	Yao	China	Yao (Mien, Man, Taipan)	1,580,000	11,000	1,232,000
11	Han Chinese (Hakka)	China	Wukinfu (Hakka colloquial)	14,760,000	89,000	10,776,000
12	Central Tibetan (Hsifan)	China	Zang wen (Central Tibetan)	4,359,000	400	3,139,000
13	Han Chinese (Hunanese)	China	Hsiang (Hunanese)	45,420,000	863,000	32,248,000
14	Han Chinese (Kan)	China	Kan	22,710,000	1,363,000	14,989,000
15	Nosu	China	Nosu	1,135,000	57,000	715,000

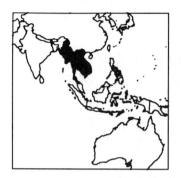

INDOCHINA PEOPLES

The Indochina cluster of unevangelized peoples, numbering more than 140 million persons, is scattered throughout the five southeast Asian nations of Vietnam, Cambodia, Laos, Thailand and Myanmar (formerly Burma).

This population complex is united by a long history of interaction through trade, socio-cultural development and warfare.

Most of the people in this area are Buddhist. Ministries to these peoples are often based in the only open country in the region: Thailand. From this strategic Indochinese center, a variety of ministries can be devised and projected into the more restricted sectors of the region.

Ten of the largest and least evangelized Indochina peoples are identified on the map on page 132. A closer look at one of these peoples, the Khmer of Cambodia, is also provided.

The Khmer of Cambodia

The Khmer people live primarily in the nation of Cambodia, though an additional million Khmer live in Vietnam. The capital of the People's Republic of Cambodia is Phnom Penh. In Cambodia, the Khmer make up the dominant population, with more than 6.5 million. The total population of the Khmer people is difficult to ascertain, due to the decades of war in the region—a war which took its heaviest toll in this small country.

It is difficult to understand the plight of the Khmer people without a glimpse into the recent history of Cambodia. Over the past century, Cambodia has repeatedly been the victim of competing foreign powers. In 1864, Cambodia first came under foreign control when France took power. French political control lasted until after World War II, when Cambodia became an autonomous state within the French Union. In 1953, Cambodia received its independence from France, and the next year the government of Prince Norodom Sihanouk was recognized as the legitimate authority within the country. Sihanouk's rule was eclipsed in 1970 when he was deposed by his general, Lon Nol.

Lon Nol was displaced in 1975 by the small yet potent Cambodian Communist group known as the Khmer Rouge, under the direction of Pol Pot. Pol Pot's brief rule was a reign of terror. Miserable living and working conditions throughout the country bred starvation and disease. These factors, along with the Khmer Rouge's systematic extermination of the educated and middle class and any other perceived enemies of the regime, resulted in the death of millions of Cambodians by 1979.

That year, Vietnam launched a military invasion of Cambodia. The Vietnamese drove the Khmer Rouge from power, and established a puppet Cambodian government composed largely of defectors from the Khmer Rouge. To date, the Khmer Rouge, Prince Sihanouk, and the Vietnam-backed government struggle for power.

Prior to the Communist takeover, Theravada (Hinayana) Buddhism was the state religion, but this religion was decimated during Pol Pot's rule. Although atheism has been the official practice since 1979, many Buddhist temples have been reopened.

A Bible in the Khmer language was translated in 1954, but is in short supply. Some Christian radio broadcasting in Khmer has persisted throughout the years of uncertainty in Cambodia, and may be producing further fruit.

As many as 11,000 Khmer people in Cambodia today may profess the Christian faith. But about 67% of the Khmer—four million people—have yet to hear of the gospel of Jesus Christ for the first time.

INDOCHINA PEOPLES

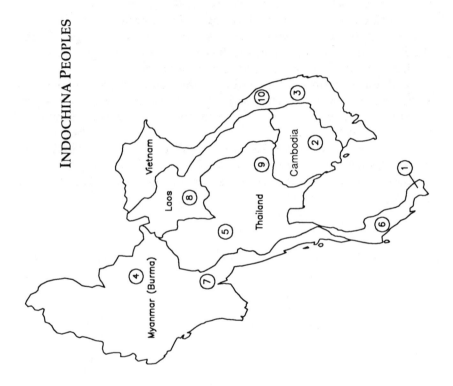

INDOCHINA PEOPLES

No.	People	Country	Language	Pop 1990	Ch affil	Unevang
1	Pattani Malay	Thailand	Malay Pattani	935,000	190	720,000
2	Khmer (Cambodian)	Cambodia	Khmer (Cambodian)	6,676,000	8,700	4,473,000
3	Khmer (Cambodian)	Vietnam	Khmer (Cambodian)	1,030,000	1,000	680,000
4	Burmese Shan (Thai Yai)	Myanmar	Shan (Ngio, Sha)	2,917,000	18,000	1,838,000
5	Northern Tai (Yuan, Phyap)	Thailand	Tai (Kammyang, Myang)	5,298,000	27,000	3,232,000
6	Southern Tai (Pak Thai)	Thailand	Tai Orkhon (Southern)	3,120,000	19,000	1,621,000
7	Burmese (Myen)	Myanmar	Bama (Burmese)	26,293,000	45,000	12,884,000
8	Lao (Laotian Tai, Lao-Lu)	Laos	Lao (Laotian Tai)	2,534,000	76,000	1,090,000
9	Lao (Laotian Tai, Isan)	Thailand	Lao (Phu lao, Isan)	14,026,000	126,000	5,190,000
10	Vietnamese (Annamese)	Vietnam	Quoc-ngu (Vietnamese)	58,375,000	4,256,000	17,513,000

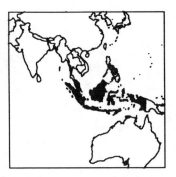

INDO-MALAYSIAN PEOPLES

The Indo-Malaysian population complex stretches from the Malay peninsula to the eastern end of the Indonesian archipelago. Though the majority of the peoples in this region are racially Malay and religiously Muslim, some of the Indo-Malaysian peoples pre-date Malay immigration, and are of aboriginal Austro-Asiatic descent.

While the governments of Indonesia and Malaysia claim widespread allegiance to Islam, research discloses a syncretistic blend of religious faiths, including animism, mysticism, and traces of Hinduism and Buddhism under a veneer of Islam.

From the perspective of nonresidential missions, the urban capital for reaching the peoples of the Indo-Malaysian complex is Singapore. Other regional centers for projecting a nonresidential witness into the region would include Manila, Bangkok and the Australian cities of Melbourne, Sidney and Canberra. From any or all of these various urban centers, teams of nonresidential missionaries would be able to interact as a common unit, linked together by computer telecommunications, and able to work together to motivate Christians. One of the keys to ministry is cooperating closely with indigenous Christian individuals and agencies within Indonesia and Malaysia.

Fifteen of the largest Indo-Malaysian peoples are identified on the map on page 136. A more detailed look at one of these peoples, the Minangkabau of Indonesian Sumatra, is also provided.

The Minangkabau of Indonesia

Most of the 6.7 million Minangkabau (Minang) live in the Padang Highlands south of Batak in the province of West Sumatra on the north Indonesian island of Sumatra, where they comprise more than 80% of the population.

Hundreds of thousands of Minang have migrated to other provinces of Sumatra (especially Riau, Djambi and North Sumatra). They are usually a conspicuous minority in cities throughout Indonesia because of their success in commerce and their high positions in government.

Altogether, Minang account for nearly four percent of the population of Indonesia. According to *Ethnologue*, another 125,000

Minangkabau live in the peninsular Malaysian state of Negri Sembilan, an island area near Melaka.

Unlike traditional Islamic groups, the Minangkabau have retained their pre-Islamic custom of matrilineal descent and inheritance. A wife remains with her maternal relatives after marriage. Her husband has no home of his own, but lives in his mother's home and visits his wife periodically. Names, privileges, and property are derived from the mother's side.

In addition to rice grown for food, pepper and coffee are grown for export. Gardening for trade is important in the well-watered and fertile volcanic soils of the northwestern part of West Sumatra, near Bukit Tinggi, but much less so in the relatively poor soils farther south, near Batang Kapas. Land is crowded in the fertile areas of the north.

The Minangkabau people are reputed to be highly resistant to missionary incursions into their region. As a result, less than .02% of the Minangkabau people—only about 1200 persons—have accepted Christianity. The vast majority are Sunni Muslim.

Although Minangkabau remains a vital language, it has only limited literature. Only portions of the New Testament have been translated into the Minangkabau language, and this was completed as late as 1980. There is a newspaper and radio station in the capital city of Jakarta on Java island, where at least 500,000 Minangkabau live, though no radio broadcasting in the Minangkabau language reaches Western Sumatra.

About 78% of the Minangkabau—more than five million people—are without any witness to Christ.

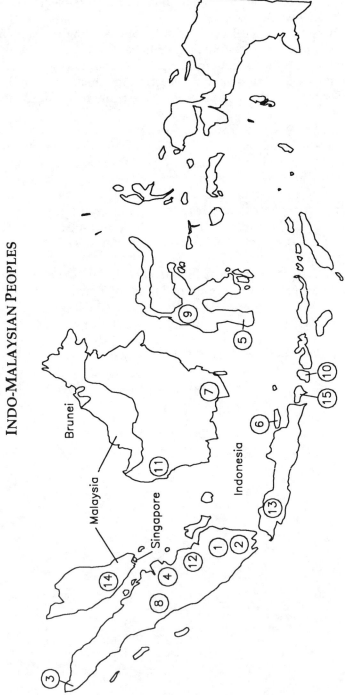

INDO-MALAYSIAN PEOPLES

INDO-MALAYSIAN PEOPLES

No.	People	Country	Language	Pop 1990	Ch affil	Unevang
1	Komering (Ogan)	Indonesia	Komering (Ogan)	1,083,000	20	996,000
2	Lamponger (Lampungese)	Indonesia	Lampung (Lampungese)	1,173,000	20	1,067,000
3	Achehnese (Aceh, Atjeh)	Indonesia	Aceh (Banda)	3,487,000	300	2,629,000
4	Bazaar Low Malay Creole	Indonesia	Pasar Malayu	1,264,000	100	1,049,000
5	Makassarese (Macassar)	Indonesia	Macassar	3,069,000	100	2,517,000
6	Madurese	Indonesia	Bankalau (Madurese)	11,332,000	178,000	9,066,000
7	Banjarese	Indonesia	Banjar	1,435,000	20	1,134,000
8	Minangkabau	Indonesia	Minangkabau	6,679,000	1,300	5,210,000
9	Buginese (Bugis)	Indonesia	Bugis	4,835,000	48,000	3,433,000
10	Sasak	Indonesia	Sasak	2,068,000	1,200	1,468,000
11	Malay (Coast Malay)	Indonesia	Malay	1,805,000	400	1,246,000
12	Jambinese Malay (Batin)	Indonesia	Jambina (Jambinese)	1,282,000	20	846,000
13	Sundanese	Indonesia	Sundanese	24,550,000	198,000	12,030,000
14	Malay (Melaju, Melayu)	Malaysia	Malay	5,601,000	1,100	2,689,000
15	Balinese	Indonesia	Balinese	3,777,000	40,000	1,435,000

Tying teams together

Each of the twelve population complexes described above is related through language, culture, history or religion. Nonresidential missionaries can greatly enhance the effectiveness of their ministry to any individual segment within one of the complexes by coordinating their efforts and forming an alliance.

The concept of teamwork to serve unevangelized complexes solves a number of potential problems. Along with building resource networks and providing accountability, a team provides the important role of spiritual support and vocational fellowship for one another. Linking together teams of nonresidential missionaries by computerized telecommunications, telephones and fax machines allows them to work in concert—even over great distances.

For example, a team of nonresidential missionaries seeking to reach the Arabic world may be scattered in locations from London to Cyprus and elsewhere within the Arabic complex. With the use of discrete communications systems, a nonresidential missionary in London can draw from the on-site contacts of a colleague surveying the situation within a closed country, and then arrange to recruit personnel in a third or even fourth country by the same means.

A final, practical by-product of the team approach to reaching complexes of peoples is that it provides an excellent organizational structure for administration. Each of the twelve teams has a leader, and meets on a regular basis for accountability and support. The twelve team leaders are then able to convene annually with the "home office" staff for purposes of reporting and further program development.

While communications systems are crucial for tying together nonresidential missionary teams, there is ultimately no substitute for periodic team meetings that include strategy planning, spiritual formation, evaluation and coordination.

As the months and years pass by, each nonresidential missionary increasingly finds his or her ministry intertwined with that of dedicated co-workers. Though each nonresidential missionary retains his own distinct assignment, it gradually becomes apparent that in God's economy, each work complements the other like the colorful, shifting patterns of a kaleidoscope.

APPENDICES

An expanded definition[1]

PLEASE DO NOT BE PUT OFF BY THIS CATALOGUE below. It is not a definition of a "supermissionary" with superhuman abilities. Regard it as you would a new city road map, a new telephone directory, or a new college text book. It is a careful definition of, or guide to, a new concept: the nonresidential missionary—a committed Christian worker or couple who want to serve an unevangelized population segment in a restricted part of the world.

This, therefore, is a list of emphases, aspects, steps, stages or activities that should characterize the nonresidential missionary. Any ordinary missionary or couple from any country is capable of filling this bill. The missionary does not have to engage in all possible evangelistic activities alone—but must check that somebody does.

It is, in fact, a list of a number of steps to take, or aspects of mission to embrace. The list of emphases or aspects is divided into 12 major categories or dimensions in the left column. The second column gives 82 characteristics or descriptors (descriptive nouns, verbs or adjectives describing who the missionary is or what he does). Each is then expanded and explained in a phrase that follows.

CALLED

1	*called*	Called to follow Christ across today's world.
2	*missionary*	A missionary working within the Christian world mission.
3	*foreign*	Most of the time, political frontiers must be crossed and entrance is as an alien or foreigner.
4	*cross-cultural*	Ministry is cross-cultural, from a home culture to a different culture.
5	*evangelizer*	Primary role is as evangelizer, among unevangelized populations.
6	*global*	Globally oriented, the missionary combs the world for other cooperators.

---

1   Reprinted by permission from *700 Plans to Evangelize the World*, David Barrett and James Reapsome, eds., (Birmingham, Alabama: New Hope, 1988).

7	*professional*	Both spouses are professional foreign missionaries.
8	*career*	This vocation is a career, possibly or probably for life.
9	*monovocational*	Though secular skills may come into play, mission or ministry is the overarching vocation.
10	*full-time*	Considers the ministry as full-time work, not a part-time interest.
11	*legal*	In any country visited, obeys the laws concerning overt evangelism.
12	*nonpolitical*	Apolitical and secure from future state hostility, evictions or bannings.
13	*nontraditional*	As traditional residential mission is impossible, becomes nontraditional.
14	*nonresidential*	Unable to reside in target segment, he becomes nonresidential.
15	*mobile*	Resident with family 70% of the time, remains mobile and flexible.

APPOINTED

16	*recruited*	Is recruited by a foreign mission board, agency, church or support body.
17	*selected*	Is tested for vocation and qualifications and then selected for service.
18	*trained*	In missionary learning centers, receives training in missions and missiology.
19	*appointed*	Is appointed by a board as one of their recognized missionaries.
20	*sent*	Is employed and sent by a board or sending body on mission.
21	*supported*	Is subsequently supported by his board regularly (money, aid, prayer, travel).

MATCHED-UP

22	*targeting*	Holds discussions to locate a target population (people, city, or country).
23	*matched-up*	Talents and vocation are matched with possible segments.
24	*focused*	Finally focuses in on one single unevangelized population segment.
25	*concentrated*	The work becomes a concentrated evangelizing ministry avoiding diversions.

| 26 | *commissioned* | The board and church commission him or her to this new ministry. |

RESEARCH

27	*language-learning*	Learns the language (market fluency) and wins wide credibility.
28	*studying*	Masters the segment: studies, maps, books, bibliographies, reports, tapes.
29	*consulting*	Compiles a list of consultants and centers with expertise on the segment.
30	*research*	Does research on (makes new discoveries about) his target population.
31	*specializing*	Takes vernacular newspapers and journals, and joins specialist societies.

NETWORKING

32	*surveying*	Surveys the entire spectrum of Christian activities within the segment.
33	*recognizing*	Recognizes, and becomes aligned with, all involved Christians.
34	*cooperating*	Actively cooperates with them, and influences them to cooperate with each other.
35	*networking*	Documents the existing network, becomes a major node, makes it a team.
36	*team-player*	Forges a *de facto* team out of all working for the segment.
37	*informing*	Develops a wide-ranging information network and keeps the team informed.
38	*catalyzing*	Where necessary, serves as a catalyzer, urging new work and new approaches.
39	*contextualizing*	Helps the network honor the global context of all segments and their interests.

STRATEGIZING

40	*biblical*	Studies and emulates biblical strategic roles (Apostle Paul, et al).
41	*discerning*	Analyzes and discerns bridges and barriers to the gospel in the segment.
42	*strategizing*	Works out, privately and through the network, an overall strategy.
43	*coordinating*	Coordinates any other approaches or ministries when necessary.

44	*communicating*	Even when isolated, communicates continually via phone, modem, electronic mail.
45	*translating*	Circulates strategic concepts translated into the language.
46	*prioritizing*	Assists others in the network to prioritize activities.
47	*telecommunicating*	If a laptop computer user, telecommunicates discreetly.
48	*databasing*	Uses multilingual infobases and databases, keeps up to date.
49	*updated*	Receives monthly computerized updates on the segment: literature, data, contacts.
50	*reporting*	Reports monthly to supporting agency on one short standard form or computer screen.
51	*updating*	Provides fuller updated status material regularly to base.
52	*monitoring*	Tracks and monitors the segment's unevangelized status continually.
53	*calendaring*	Keeps track of future dates and ensures items occur on schedule.

INTERCEDING

54	*praying*	Gets the network praying that the AD 2000 overarching objective may be met.
55	*prayer-mobilizing*	Mobilizes prayer partners in any country where this is possible.
56	*interceding*	Develops a ministry of informed intercession by home churches and agencies.

EVANGELIZING

57	*evangelizing*	The main task is evangelizing, in its 200-or-so distinct dimensions and methods.
58	*goal-oriented*	The goal is that everyone in the segment become evangelized by AD 2000.
59	*responsible*	Accepts responsibility to see to it that the whole network achieves this goal.
60	*future-oriented*	Orients ministry to both AD 2000, and "AD2000 and beyond."
61	*teaching*	Main teaching is, informally, on how the network can achieve this goal.

MINISTERING

62	*ministering*	Continually draws up new ministry options and motivates the team to implement them.
63	*proclaiming*	Sees to it that by all methods a continuous proclamation of Christ goes on.
64	*seed-sowing*	The goal is to see adequate Scripture distribution, broadcasting, literature, etc.
65	*disciple-making*	The goal is at least 100 new disciples made in this segment by AD 2000.
66	*church-planting*	The goal is four or five new beachhead churches planted and leaders trained by AD 2000.
67	*indigenizing*	Encourages emergence of new indigenous expressions of Christianity in the segment.

IMPLEMENTING

68	*visiting*	Visits the target area as a tourist or for secular events (conferences, etc).
69	*entrepreneurial*	Creative and versatile, exploits opportunities as and when they occur.
70	*facilitating*	As a facilitator, actively assists others to perform their roles.
71	*locating*	Advises on possible location of tentmakers or others resident in the segment.
72	*mobilizing*	As a mobilizer, locates new resources and additional personnel.
73	*implementing*	As an implementer, ensures all agreed steps are actually implemented.
74	*conflict-avoiding*	Avoids conflict between the segment's interests and outside Christian work.

ADVOCATING

75	*relating*	Maintains good relations with secular, religious and Christian authorities.
76	*advocating*	Serves as advocate, anywhere, for the segment and their evangelization.
77	*lobbying*	When necessary, lobbies energetically on behalf of the segment.
78	*low-key*	Aware of the dangers of publicity, keeps a low profile.
79	*sensitizing*	Alerts and sensitizes the network to needs for confidentiality and security.

TRAINING

80	*equipping*	Sees to it that indigenous leadership emerges equipped for ministry.
81	*training*	Assists with training seminars for new nonresidential missionaries anywhere.
82	*recruiting*	Keeps alert to recruit nonresidential missionaries for segments elsewhere.

How to do research on population targets

WHILE THERE IS NO SUBSTITUTE FOR LENGTHY and intensive nonresidential missionary training, trainees can take some preliminary steps to become better acquainted with a population segment or city. While the type of in-depth research outlined in Chapter Seven may require database retrieval systems inaccessible to the amateur investigator, much can be learned from more common sources.

As Allan Starling demonstrates in the *Peoplesfile Index*, a great deal of preliminary research can be done in a moderately-equipped Christian reference library. The steps outlined in Starling's essay below should prove adequate for purposes of matching a missionary candidate with an unevangelized population target. Once an assignment is secured, the nonresdential missionary can take the next steps of training and deployment.

Finding hidden peoples in the library[2]

> The whole earth was of one language and of one speech . . .
> And the Lord said: . . . Come, let us go down and there confuse
> their language so that they cannot understand one another's
> speech. So the Lord scattered them . . . upon the face of all the
> earth" (Genesis 11:1,7,8).

When God does a job, he does it well! Today, thousands of years after Babel, the world is still scattered with such a confusion of peoples and languages that even the experts find it hard to agree on just how many there are and how they are related. The very names of these groups are "confused"—one group may be known by as many as five different names. Yet God's love extends to each people, and he is "not willing that any should perish."

As followers of Christ, we have our orders to reach all these peoples with the good news of the gospel. In recent years, Christians around the world have become increasingly aware of the need to identify these groups and to ask a number of questions: "Who are they? Where are they? How many of them are there? What do they believe? Is anyone reaching out to them with the Gospel?"

---

2   Adapted from Allan Starling's *Peoplesfile Index* (Pasadena, California: Global Mapping International, 1986). Used by permission of the author.

Let us assume that you have heard about a people called the AFAR, reported to live somewhere in eastern Africa. You feel that God wants you to be involved in reaching them with the gospel. How can you find out more about them? Where do you start?

Fortunately, much of the information is out there, waiting for someone like you to find it. Think of it as a treasure hunt. All you need is a set of clues, some time, and a heap of patience and persistence. I would be most delighted to accompany you, so let us do it together.

PART I: Establishing the clues

Before we start on our treasure hunt, we need some clues. Those clues about the AFAR can be obtained through the *Peoplesfile Index* and the three publications it references. If these publications are not available at your local library, you can check with mission offices, Bible School libraries, or order them from the addresses given elsewhere.

Checking the *Peoplesfile Index*, we find clues about the AFAR:

Clue #1: All three source publications use AFAR as the primary name, with DANAKIL as a secondary name.

Clue #2: The AFAR are reported as being UNEVANGELIZED.

Clue #3: Gospel Recordings has made RECORDINGS of the Afar language.

Clue #4: BIBLE PORTIONS are available in Afar.

Clue #5: The group is in the following countries: DJIBOUTI, ETHIOPIA, and SOMALIA.

Clue #6: The group is known as AFAR, ADAL, AFARAF, AFARAFA and DANAKIL.

Checking the *Ethnologue*, we make some additional discoveries:

Clue #7: The AFAR are a NOMADIC people.

Clue #8: SAHO is a related, but distinct group.

Clue #9: The following agencies are working among the AFAR: SIM, CMML, OPC, RSM, ECMY. We will find the meaning of these acronyms later.

Checking the *Unreached Peoples Annuals* (Clue #2) we further find:

Clue #10: UNREACHED PEOPLES '79 has an expanded description of the AFAR.

Clue #11: The AFAR are a MUSLIM people.

Let us use some of these clues to find more information about the AFAR. As I have mentioned, the three publications referenced by *Peoplesfile Index* may not be found in most public libraries. Other references, however, may either be found in our library, obtained through inter-library loan by our friendly librarian, or purchased. Now, we are finally ready for the library.

PART II: Searching the library

We need to remind ourselves of some basics. First, do not expect to find all the resources mentioned here in every library. Obviously, the more you find, the better, but even one or two of them might yield a rich amount of information.

If possible, find a university library or main city library, or perhaps one at a mission office. Some of the resources may only be found in American libraries. Even if you can only find a few of the resources mentioned, you might still be able to build a good picture of the people you are researching.

Also remember that, unless you have a library card, you will not be able to borrow books, but since many libraries have photocopy machines, let's take plenty of change for making copies.

We need to give ourselves plenty of time at the library—a whole day if possible. "Finding" a people isn't always easy. It will take some patient research, and we are going to have to look in several places.

Let us break our search into a number of steps:

Step 1:   Determine the search procedure.

We will use this procedure in each of the following steps. Unless we are looking for a large group, chances are we will not find what we want immediately, because the information will be hidden in some volume or periodical. (Is that why they call them "Hidden" peoples?) We start with the specific and move to broader categories as necessary. Here are the categories we chose in our search for the AFAR:

   a.   Afar, Danakil (clue #1)
   b.   Nomads (clue #7)
   c.   Saho (clue #8)
   d.   Muslim or Islam (clue #11)
   e.   Ethnology
   f.   Anthropology
   g.   Djibouti, Ethiopia, Somalia (clue #5)
   h.   Other names for Afar (Danakil) (clue #6)

Step 2:   Check the *National Geographic Magazine Index.*

Published by National Geographic Society, Washington, D.C. 20036, USA, the index of articles from 1947 to 1983 tells us of an article called "THE DANAKIL: Nomads of Ethiopia's Wasteland" in their Feb. 1970 issue. We will also enjoy their usual high-quality colored pictures.

Step 3:   Check the Index Volume of the *Encyclopedia Britannica*.

The *Encyclopedia* has a surprising amount of information about peoples and countries. In their Index Volume, under *AFAR*, we see that they have an article entitled SAHO-AFAR. There is more information under "ETHIOPIA: The People." We are also told that the Afar are Sunni Muslims, and that we can get more info under "ISLAM."

Step 4:   Check *Muslim Peoples: A World Ethnographic Survey*, edited by Richard V. Weekes.

The second edition, revised and expanded to two volumes, contains maps showing general location of Muslim groups, and documents 190 Ethnic and/or linguistic groups, either totally or partially Muslim. Volume 1, page 10, includes an article on the AFAR and a bibliography for further reading. An appendix, giving Muslim ethnic groups by country, shows us that the AFAR form one of nineteen Muslim groups in Ethiopia. We already know that the AFAR are Muslim, (clue #11), which led us to take this step.

Step 5:   Check Danbury Press' 20-volume set of *Peoples of the Earth*.

Although this is out of print, our particular library fortunately has a set. In addition to general articles, each volume contains many thumbnail sketches and pictures of people groups. Continuing our quest for AFAR information, we find that Volume 2, page 22, has an article on the DANAKIL and SOHO (clue #8), which includes maps and pictures.

Step 6:   Check in the 20-volume set of *The Illustrated Encyclopedia of Mankind*.

Published by Marshall Cavendish Ltd., 58 Old Compton St., London, W1V5PA, the *Illustrated Encyclopedia* includes more than 500 peoples and cultures. Yes, the AFAR are there too! There is an article with colored pictures on page 12 of volume one.

Step 7:   Check the *Library of Congress Subject Headings*.

These large bound volumes, kept in most libraries, show the subject headings used in the card catalog system. Even if our library does not use the Library of Congress system (most in USA now do), this step is still useful. The headings in bold type are those used in the Card Catalog. Other names in the volume are related topics.

Under AFAR, we actually find AFAR LANGUAGE (PJ2421) listed as a heading. Because our library uses Library of Congress codes, we can now go straight to the "PJ" section in the shelves and look for related books. If the library used the Dewey Decimal System, we would simply jot down the headings to use in the next step.

Sorry, there are no books we can use under the "PJ" section in our library, so let us look under a broader topic. There are a number of headings under MUSLIM, and under ETHIOPIA we find ETHIOPIAN LANGUAGES (PJ8991-9). Even though we are unsuccessful once again, we keep a note of the headings to use in the next few steps.

Step 8:   Check the Card Catalog file.

Let us remember to follow the procedure we set up in Step One, aided by the subject headings we found in the last step. Whether the catalog file uses Dewey Decimal or Library of Congress codes, the procedure is the same. As soon as we find one volume in the card catalog that looks promising, we look for it, as well as for other related volumes near it, on that section of the shelves.

Step 9:   Check the *Subject Guide to Books in Print*.

The librarian shows us where to find these large bound volumes. Once again, using our set procedure and our list of subject headings we find the names of several books in print related to the AFAR.

Step 10:   Check the *Linguistic Bibliography*, edited by J. Beylsmit.

This contains a listing of "all" the descriptions of known languages. Although the articles and books referred to may be technical in nature, many times they will include a section on the speakers of the language and give additional useful information.

Step 11:   Check the MARC (MAchine Readable Catalog) Fiche.

If you are not familiar with fiche, they are a form of microfilm, but on 3 x 5 "cards." Our library has a microfiche reader handy. By the way, this "MARC" is not related to the MARC which is publisher of this book and a division of World Vision International.

We check the Author/Title index first, once again using our set procedure. We come up with "Afar Depression in Ethiopia" #838 e 29. Next, we check microfiche number 838, square e 29, and see a description of a book that is not at all what we want. If it had been, we could have written down the Library of Congress and Dewey classification which are given below the description. Oh well, we can't win them all!

Step 12:   Check the periodicals guides.

With our librarian's help, we find a number of periodical indices in our library: *Readers Guide to Periodical Literature*, *Christian Periodical Index*, and the *Social Sciences Index*.

Step 13: Check the U.S. Department of State's Bureau of Public Affairs' *Background Notes.*

We can get these from the Superintendent of Documents, U.S. Government Printing Office, Washington DC 20402 USA. We ask for a single copy by country name, or by subscription. The notes give an overview of the geography, government, policies, economy, history and people of the country.

Step 14: Check *Human Relations Area Files* (HRAF).

This is only possible if you live in the USA, and have access to certain major universities. The files contain detailed information on approximately 400 different cultures.

Step 15: Talk to the Reference Librarian.

Before leaving the library, we talk to the librarian and explain what we are looking for, and what we have already found. The more we know, the more the librarian can help us. (Several of the clues for this treasure hunt come from Harry Fuchigami at the library of the US Center for World Mission in Pasadena.)

PART III: Looking further

We are finished at the library, but our research is not complete. Other people, organizations and publications will aid our search.

Step 16: Check mission agencies working in or near our people group.

Remembering that missionaries are busy people, we do our homework first, and then send them a copy of our findings, along with specific questions. If we demonstrate that we are serious, they are more likely to spend time digging out additional information or checking what we have.

First, we check the *Ethnologue* for the full names of the missions working with our group (clue #8). Here they are:

a. CMML = Christian Missions in Many Lands (Plymouth Brethren)
b. ECMY = Evangelical Lutheran Church in Ethiopia
c. OPC = Orthodox Presbyterian Church
d. RSM = Red Sea Mission
e. SIM = SIM International (formerly Sudan Interior Mission)

We are surprised to find five groups working among the AFAR. Remember that the definition of an unevangelized population segment is based on the strength of the indigenous community of believing Christians in that group, rather than the amount of work being done in that group. We also note that these people are both nomadic and

Muslim. Further note the *Ethnologue* explanation that the names represent "agencies working in the . . . group, or which have produced published Scripture . . . space does not allow explanation of the kind of work of each agency."

To get the mission addresses and/or find other possible agencies, we then check MARC's *Missions Handbook* or the *UK Christian Handbook*, published by the Evangelical Alliance, 186 Kennington Park Rd., London SE11 4BT. Both handbooks contain a listing by the names of the organizations as well as by country.

Step 17: Learn more about the geographic areas where our group is located. Some of these references may be in your library. You may have to order or borrow others.

a. *Operation World* by Patrick Johnstone. STL Publications, P.O. Box 28, Waynesboro, GA 30830, USA; or P.O. Box 48, Bromley, Kent, England.

This survey of the basic prayer needs of each country of the world is backed by information on population, ethnic groups, economy, religions and political situations. The fourth edition is completely rewritten.

b. *World Christian Encyclopedia* edited by David B. Barrett, Oxford University Press, USA.

"The heart of the Encyclopedia is a detailed, country-by-country survey of Christianity and other religions . . . including political, demographic, linguistic, ethnic and cultural data . . .", and much more. Checking under "Djibouti" and "Ethiopia," we find a lot of information about these countries. We also get some specific information about the AFAR, finding, for instance, that Danakil are 35.1 percent of the population of Djibouti and 0.9 percent in Ethiopia. There is also a picture of an Afar man in the country of Djibouti.

Finding the name "AFAR" in the index on page 988, we see a code CMT33z. This leads us to page 113, which yields the information that they are "other Cushitic," TanBrown, and an alternate name for Danakil. The global table on page 787 tells us they are part of a larger grouping of 25 people groups speaking 20 languages. Among other statistics, we note that this major grouping is only 1.41% Christian, and since the word "Christian" here represents a broad category, we conclude that there are extremely few evangelicals among them.

c. *World Christianity Series*, published by MARC, a division of World Vision International, 919 W. Huntington Drive, Monrovia, California, 91016, USA.

A series of concise paperbacks, each giving a survey of the status of the Christian faith in a particular region. Currently available are books on Central America and the Caribbean, Eastern Asia, the Middle East, South Asia, Oceania, Eastern Europe, Southern Africa, and South Central Africa.

d. Other references, including *Area Handbooks, Encyclopedia of the Third World, Times Atlas,* and *National Geographic Atlas of the World.*

Step 18: Check with agencies doing research on the peoples of the world.

In most cases, this can be a two-way street. Not only can you request specific information, you can also help to update or correct existing data. Some groups have questionnaires for use in gathering data.

a. Gospel Recordings, Field Division, 122 Glendale Boulevard, Los Angeles, CA 90026 USA.

Request the latest recorded language directory for a specific country; ask for catalog of available audio tools (records, cassettes, players); obtain information on a specific recorded language.

b. The Editor, *Ethnologue,* 7500 W. Camp Wisdom Road, Dallas, TX 75236 USA.

Use their questionnaire to supply information; order the *Ethnologue* from the bookstore at above address.

c. Global Mapping International, P.O. Box 25399, Colorado Springs, CO 80936-5399 USA.

Use their Research Data Forms to supply information pertaining to the peoples of the world; Ask for information and maps, and especially about their *People Group Profiles.* They may even have one on the AFAR!

d. Research institutes located at the U.S. Center for World Missions at 1605 Elizabeth Street, Pasadena, CA 91104 USA.

Institute of Chinese Studies; Institute of Global Urban Studies; Institute of Hindu Studies; Institute of Japanese Studies; Institute of Latin American Studies; Institute of Tribal Studies; and the Samuel Zwemer Institute for Muslim Studies. Check for specific information on people groups; ask about seminars and courses offered; request descriptions of available materials.

e. WEC International Research Office, Bulstrode, Gerrards Cross, Bucks SL9 8SZ, U.K.

Ask about information on microfiche equivalent of up to 200,000 pages of background information on languages and countries.

f. MARC, a ministry of World Vision International, 919 W. Huntington Drive, Monrovia, CA 91016 USA.

g. World Evangelization Research Center, the Foreign Mission
    Board of the Southern Baptist Convention, P.O. Box 6767,
    Richmond, VA 23230 USA.

What now?

Now that we have the information, what are we going to do with
it? That is a question that only you, with the Lord's guidance, can
answer. There are, however, several things you can consider:

- HELP other agencies update their files by sharing
  new information you discover with them. They, in
  turn, will share it with others who need it.
- PRAY for the peoples of the world. Adopt a group
  for specific prayer.
- ASK the Lord how he wants you to be involved in
  serving "your" group.

My prayer is that the "Lord of the harvest" will "thrust forth
laborers" into that part of the harvest field that includes "your" people
group.

Glossary[3]

AD 2000 and Beyond. A slogan used to encapsulate the goal of completing the evangelization of the world by the year 2000 and keeping it evangelized in the subsequent years.

AD 2000 plan. A global plan or non-global plan publicly announced on the part of a church, denomination, mission, or parachurch or service agency to achieve a specific evangelization goal or goals by or around the year 2000.

advocacy. The process of championing a particular unevangelized population segment, especially if voiceless or neglected, and continually seeking opportunities to present its case for a larger share of Christian resources.

beachhead. The initial planting of indigenous fellowships in an otherwise unreached people or unevangelized population segment.

Christian World. In the 3-tier schema, this is World C, consisting of all who individually are Christians.

closed country. A country whose government or regime has closed it to some major form or forms of Christian ministry from outside, usually resident foreign missionaries, visiting evangelists, or freely distributed scriptures, Christian literature, tapes or videos or films, or other Christian influences from outside.

closing country. A country still open to outside Christian influences but whose increasing restrictions suggest it may become closed within a few months or years.

country. A term covering both (a) sovereign nations, and (b) nonsovereign territories (dependencies or colonies) which are not integral parts of larger parent nations.

E%. A computed estimate of the percentage of persons in a particular population segment (world, country, people, city) who have become evangelized, by or at a certain date.

---

3   Selected definitions reprinted by permission from David Barrett and Todd Johnson's *Our Globe and How to Reach It* (Birmingham, Alabama: New Hope, 1990).

ethnolinguistic people. A distinct homogeneous ethnic or racial group within a single country, speaking its own language (one single mother tongue). A large people spread across two, three, four or several countries is treated here as being two, three, four or several distinct ethnolinguistic peoples.

evangelism. The church's organized activity of spreading the gospel, in circumstances it can control, in contrast to witness which is the normal term for the informal, spontaneous, unorganized sharing of their faith by individual Christians in circumstances they do not control.

evangelization. (a) The whole process of spreading the good news of the Kingdom of God; (b) the extent to which the good news has been spread; (c) the extent of awareness of Christianity, Christ, and the gospel.

evangelize. To spread the good news of Christ, with signs following, in both supernatural power and compassionate deed, to preach, to persuade, to call to faith in Christ.

Evangelized Non-Christian World. In the 3-tier schema, this is World B, which consists of all non-Christians who have nevertheless become evangelized.

evangelized persons. Individuals who have had adequate opportunity or opportunities to hear the gospel and to respond to it.

fax. Facsimile transmission of digitized pictures or text over telephone lines.

frontier missionary. A full-time foreign or cross-cultural missionary who works among an unreached people, an unevangelized population segment or in World A.

frontier people. An alternate term for an unreached minipeople.

global evangelization movement. A term describing the vast number of distinct agencies and plans directed towards world evangelization which have proliferated across the world since the year 1900.

hidden people. An alternate term for an unreached minipeople.

interdenominational. Occurring between or among or common to several or many denominations; accountable to several denominations, or partially or completely controlled by them.

itinerant. Adjective describing an evangelist, missionary, or other church worker whose ministry involves being continually on the move from one city or people or country to the next.

kaleidoscopic. Multi-faceted, many-featured, constantly changing.

language set. A grouping of language units sharing from 35-75% common vocabulary.

language unit. A grouping of idioms whose speech communities share from 75-95% common vocabulary.

limited-access country. A country whose government or regime limits access by alien foreign missionaries wishing to reside, usually by small or decreasing quotas or progressively shorter residence permits; see *closing country*.

matching up or **matching.** The process of linking or linking up a particular unreached people or unevangelized population segment with a specific ministry or mission agency or missionary; in particular, with a nonresidential missionary whose vocation it would be to see that the segment becomes evangelized by AD2000.

megacity. A metropolis or other city with a population of over one million persons.

megapeople. An ethnolinguistic people speaking a single mother tongue whose population numbers over one million.

minipeople. The largest people group within which the gospel can spread as a church-planting movement without encountering barriers of understanding or acceptance.

ministry options. A list of possible or potential ministries or missionary or evangelistic approaches that a nonresidential missionary draws up, which he or she considers could be undertaken by a large variety of agents and agencies on behalf of his target segment.

monovocational. In contrast to bivocational persons, monovocational persons describes missionaries whose main or only vocation and profession is full-time Christian service with particular emphasis on the ministry of evangelization and evangelism that results in churches.

mother tongue. The first language spoken in an individual's home in his early or earliest childhood; one's first language or native language.

multichanneling. A mode of operation which accepts the present unsatisfactory multiciplicity of global plans on the part of hundreds of mission agencies, recognizing that their stand-alone nature at least serves as insurance against multiple or overall failure.

nation. A politically-organized nationality with independent, self-governening, autonomous existence as a sovereign country or nation-state, hence eligible for membership in the United Nations.

people or people group. A significantly large grouping of individuals who perceive themselves to have a common affinity for one another because of their shared language, religion, ethnicity, residence, occupation, class or caste, situation, etc. or combination of these. Examples of people groups are ethnolinguistic peoples, minipeoples, unimax peoples, micropeoples, metropeoples, sociopeoples and bridge peoples. The full definition, a result of a meeting of mission executives in Chicago in March of 1982, is preserved under minipeople allowing a broader meaning for people group.

people movement. The spread of the gospel among a people in such a way that all individuals in that group are presented with an opportunity to know Christ; usually accompanied by significant response.

restricted access country. A country whose government or regime restricts access by foreign missionaries wishing to reside, foreign Christians wishing to visit, or foreign Christian literature, or broadcasting, or other Christian ministries or influences.

segment. Any homogeneous subdivision of the world's population, made for purposes of understanding and analysis; the most generalized English translation of the biblical Greek word *ethnos* (usually translated "people").

segmentization. The process of dividing the world's population into meaningful small segments—usually countries, peoples, or cities—in order to assist toward their targeting and evangelization.

short-term (short-service) missionaries. Persons serving abroad as foreign missionary personnel under a recognized mission agency for a single period of from 3 to 24 months only.

targeting. In world mission, the process of a Christian worker, missionary, couple, or small team focusing in on selecting, as an object of ministry and service, one single homogeneous entity (city, people) usually termed an unevangelized population segment.

unevangelized persons. Individuals who have had no adequate opportunity to hear the gospel or respond to it; persons who are unaware of Christianity, Christ, and the gospel; those who have never heard the name of Jesus.

unevangelized population segment. A bite-sized piece or chunk of homogeneous unevangelized persons, a manageable homogeneous piece which has not yet become evangelized, which is capable of being targeted by a church, mission, agency, cooperating agencies, or an individual missionary or couple with a view to its evangelization.

Unevangelized World. In the 3-tier schema, this is World A, consisting of all non-Christians who have not been evangelized.

unfinished task. The remaining task of evangelization, as the task of the Christian church on earth, viewed as the church's responsibility within God's plan for the world; usually viewed as completing the fulfillment of Christ's Great Commission.

vehicular megalanguage. A language with a million or more speakers which acts as a trade language or *lingua franca*.

viable indigenous church. Within an ethnolinguistic people or minipeople, an indigenous community of believing Christians with adequate numbers and resources to evangelize their own people group without needing outside cross-cultural assistance.

witness. The normal term used for the informal, spontaneous, unorganized sharing of their faith, by presence, word, or deed, by individual Christians in circumcumstances they do not control; as contrasted with organized evangelism.

World A. In the 3-tier schema or representation of the earth, the unevangelized world, i.e., the world of all unevangelized individuals.

World B. In the 3-tier schema or representation of the earth, the evangelized non-Christian world, i.e., all non-Christians who have nevertheless become evangelized.

World C. In the 3-tier schema or representation of the earth, the Christian world, i.e., the world of all who individually are Christians.

world evangelization. The term used for the goal of reaching the entire world with the gospel of Christ, or of giving every people and population on Earth the opportunity to hear the gospel with understanding and to become disciples of Christ.